ELECTRONIC BRAIN GAMES

CROSSWORDS

Using Your Brain Games Pen

1. Slide the cartridge into the slot on the side of the Pen.

2. Plug the earbuds or headphones (required) into the headphone jack.

3. Press ⏻ to turn the Pen on and off.

4. Use the pencil to write. Touch objects on the page with the other end of the Brain Games Pen to hear audio and play games.

5. Press the raised button on the top of the Pen to push out more pencil lead.

6. If the lead runs out, refill with 0.7mm pencil lead. Press the raised button down completely and slide in the new lead.

7. After five minutes of inactivity, the Pen will shut off. However, if a game such as a Sudoku puzzle is being timed, the Pen will store the game results and continue to run the timer for two hours while the LED flashes slowly. Press ⏻ to wake the Pen up.

8. If batteries are low, a double beep plays and the LED starts flashing quickly.

9. If the cartridge is not installed, or if the batteries are dead, a double beep plays, the LED flashes, and the Pen shuts off.

10. To adjust the volume, touch the volume controls on this page with the Pen.

VOLUME

🔊 🔊 🔊 🔊

BRAIN GAMES

POWERED BY
SD·X
INTERACTIVE

Battery Installation

1. Open battery door with small flat-head or Phillips screwdriver.
2. Install new batteries according to +/- polarity. If batteries are not installed properly, the device will not function.
3. Replace battery door; secure with small screw.

Battery Safety

Properly dispose of used batteries. See battery manufacturer for disposal recommendations. Do not mix alkaline, standard (carbon-zinc), or rechargeable (nickel-cadmium) batteries. Do not mix old and new batteries. Only recommended batteries of the same or equivalent type should be used. Non-rechargeable batteries are not to be recharged.

Warning: Changes or modifications to this unit not expressly approved by the party responsible for compliance could void the user's authority to operate the equipment.

NOTE: This equipment has been tested and found to comply with the limits for a Class B digital device, pursuant to Part 15 of the FCC Rules. These limits are designed to provide reasonable protection against harmful interference in a residential installation. This equipment generate uses, and can radiate radio frequency energy and, if not installed and used in accordance with the instructions, may cause harmful interferenc to radio communications. However, there is no guarantee that interference will not occur in a particular installation. If this equipment does cause harmful interference to radio or television reception, which can be determined by turning the equipment off and on, the user is encourage to try to correct the interference by one or more of the following measures: Reorient or relocate the receiving antenna. Increase the separatio between the equipment and receiver. Connect the equipment into an outlet on a circuit different from that to which the receiver is connectec Consult the dealer or an experienced radio TV technician for help.

Powered by SD•X Interactive™ technology.

Puzzlers: Kelly Clark, Mark Danna, Harvey Estes, Alun Evans, Ray Hamel, Timothy Park
Illustrators: Nicole H. Lee, Jay Sato, Shavan R. Spears

7373 North Cicero Avenue   Ground Floor, 59 Gloucester Place
Lincolnwood, Illinois 60712   London W1U 8JJ

Customer Service: 1-888-724-0144 or customer_service@pilbooks.com
www.pilbooks.com | www.sdxi.com

Brain Games is a trademark of Publications International, Ltd.
SD-X Interactive is a trademark of SD-X Interactive, Inc.

Manufactured in China.

8 7 6 5 4 3 2 1

ISBN-10: 1-4127-9847-7
ISBN-13: 978-1-4127-9847-1

BOOST YOUR BRAIN POWER WITH

Crosswords

Whether you're a beginner or an old hand, the special features of the Brain Games Pen give you a great way to enjoy solving crossword puzzles.

Solving crossword puzzles has benefits besides having fun! Studies have shown that the more you exercise your brain, the better it responds. Solving crossword puzzles helps you brush up on language skills, stretch your memory, and keep your brain nimble.

A puzzle, some clues, a pencil, and an eraser. What more do you need for crossword puzzles? The Brain Games Pen! We've taken an old favorite and made some improvements that will please crossword veterans and help out beginners.

Traditional crossword puzzles come with an answer key. When a puzzle seems insolvable, a player can look in the answer key to solve an elusive clue. But if you've looked at answer keys before, you know that it's hard not to notice the other words right next to the one you looked up!

With the Brain Games Pen and the interactive crossword on each page, you'll be able to control exactly how much of a hint you'd like to access. Use the written clues and the pencil point to fill in the standard puzzle— then use the interactive crossword and the Pen when you're stumped!

Control the Pen's volume by touching the volume control buttons on the first page of this book.

The interactive crossword gives you two options:

- If you touch the Pen to a particular space, you'll hear the correct letter for that space. Touch all spaces in a word to spell the entire word.

- If you want to verify that you have the correct letter for a space, you can touch the Pen to a blue letter button on the verify bar, then touch the space where you think that letter belongs. You'll hear either "That's right," or "Keep trying."

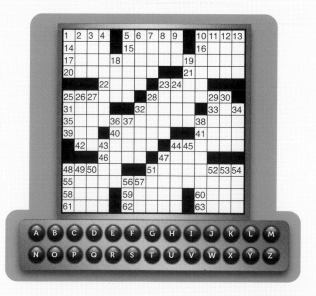

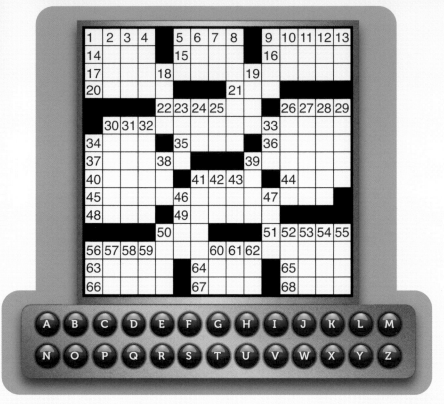

Patriotic Songs

Across

1. Emotional shock
5. Stare at the stars
9. Mr. T's squad, with "The"
14. Kind of rug
15. Most populous continent
16. Creator of Winnie the Pooh
17. 1995 hit song by TLC
20. Enjoys a bath
21. Two times five
22. Came closer to
26. Fully gratify a desire
30. Holiday song crooned by Crosby
34. "The Man Who Mistook His Wife for ___"
35. Boxer Spinks who beat Ali
36. Skins an apple
37. Sprees
39. Last name of Stallone's Rocky
40. An inert gas
41. Rocky for Stallone
44. A lot of
45. Footwear in an Elvis Presley song
48. Nile snakes
49. Must
50. One ___ time
51. Sheriff's star
56. What the answers to 17-, 30-, and 45-Across contain
63. Harvests
64. Ark builder
65. Sigh word
66. With 32-Down, newswoman Linda Ellerbee's tag line
67. Japanese wrestling
68. Title fish in a 2003 animated movie

Down

1. Containers
2. Three-layer cookie
3. She dallied with a swan
4. Speak

5. Practical joke

6. ___ Wednesday

7. Pimple

8. Defunct airline

9. Prayer ending

10. First X or O in a
3-in-a-row game

11. Yale student

12. Santa ___ winds

13. Actor/director Gibson

18. Ain't right?

19. Prefix for cure or cab

23. Shocking fish

24. Top card

25. Greek letter before sigma

26. Patron saint of sailors

27. One-celled organisms

28. Eagle's claws

29. Test that's not true/false

30. Spins

31. End a phone call

32. See 66-Across

33. Health resort

34. Addis ___ (capital of Ethiopia)

38. Naval rank: abbr.

39. Tops

41. Once again gains money
or trust

42. Poem of praise

43. Was ahead

46. "For ___ us a child is born…"

47. Traveling tramp

50. In addition

52. Actor Alda

53. Loser to Bill Clinton

54. Unit of mass

55. Old gas brand

56. With 60-Down,
"… ___ mouse?"

57. Famed KC QB Dawson

58. Mom's spouse

59. In-car location finder

60. With 56-Down,
"Are ___ a man…"

61. America's uncle

62. Korean-American
comic Margaret

Lip Service

Across

1. "Yikes"
5. Lumberyard tools
9. "Hungarian Rhapsodies" composer Franz
14. Employee's move, for short
15. "___ Silver! Away!"
16. "...an old woman who lived in ___"
17. Comfy footwear
20. Popular swimwear brand
21. Leaves the dock
22. One of Alcott's "Little Women"
24. Agnus ___ (Lamb of God)
25. Nine-digit ID org.
26. Scrooge's expletive
29. Practice boxing
31. Session: abbr.
33. Jai ___
35. Swift, compact horse
37. Exhorts
41. Shears for a hair pro
44. Foe
45. Beer foam
46. Basic seasoning
47. Harden
49. Miffed state
51. Domicile: abbr.
52. Spot of land in the Seine
55. Opening
57. Mrs. David Copperfield
59. Tinny-sounding
62. "Give a ring sometime!"
66. Griddle utensils
68. Soft Dutch cheeses
69. Repetitive learning process
70. Does a gardening chore
71. Zaps with a stun gun
72. Lith. and Ukr., formerly
73. Assistant

Down

1. Eyes, poetically
2. Dickens's Uriah
3. Like many a New England "shoppe"
4. Mount in Exodus

1	2	3	4		5	6	7	8		9	10	11	12	13
14					15					16				
17				18				19						
20						21								
			22		23		24				25			
26	27	28		29		30		31		32				
33			34		35			36		37		38	39	40
41				42					43					
44					45					46				
			47		48		49			50		51		
52	53	54		55		56		57			58			
59			60				61		62			63	64	65
66						67								
68				69						70				
71				72						73				

5. Have a good day on the links
6. Prepare to fire
7. "Swiss Family Robinson" author Johann
8. Did a cobbler's job
9. Enjoys thoroughly, as praise, slangily
10. AOL and others
11. Mets' stadium's dedicatee et al.
12. Geisha's footwear
13. Inventor and electrical engineer Nikolai
18. "___ to Joy"
19. News bit
23. Severe
26. Like a ___ in the woods
27. He played 'Hawkeye' Pierce
28. Loser to the tortoise
30. Track meet events
32. Orgs.
34. Some PCs
36. Not at all spicy
38. Equipment
39. ___ Stanley Gardner
40. Retired sound-breakers
42. Monocle
43. Extreme follies
48. Use a phone
50. Ensnare
52. Egg on
53. You can ___ horse to water...
54. Old lab burners
56. Marina sights
58. First Greek letter
60. Topmost
61. Corp. money chiefs
63. First of 13 popes
64. Classic TV's talking horse
65. Caesar's existence
67. Env. content, maybe

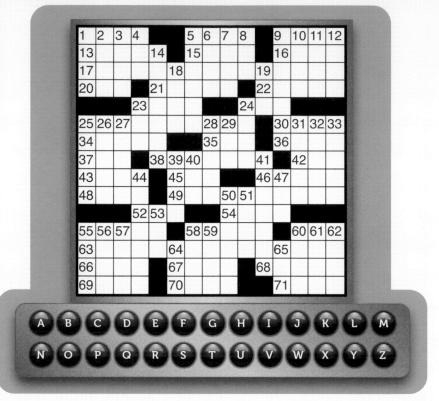

Zoo Story

Across

1. Former Cleveland pitcher Charles
5. Phony
9. Belch
13. Yearly record
15. Britishism
16. Song for Bartoli
17. Creepy person
20. Chapeau
21. Collect patiently
22. Arctic quarter
23. Pitcher
24. "Strangers ___ Train"
25. Chicken
30. Mad scientist's assistant
34. Dance in a line
35. Believer: suf.
36. Famous fiddler
37. The Greatest
38. Street swine
42. Collar
43. Father of Portnoy
45. Fifties' initials
46. Lenya
48. Lady of the haus
49. Overnight stars, in a way
52. Appliance store items: abbr.
54. Regatta sights
55. Tend to the turkey
58. Domineering
60. Auto club initials
63. Relatives of the paparazzi
66. The Shah's former country
67. Theater award
68. Sideshow attraction
69. Cereal grains
70. Max Jr. or Sr.
71. La Douce

Down

1. "Candy is dandy. . . " author
2. Magnani
3. No-see-um
4. Asian bovine
5. Sunday best
6. Powell–Loy costar

10

7. Late comedic actor Madeline
8. The mind's ___
9. Basement find
10. Mountain range
11. Rice: Ital.
12. El ___
14. Stockings, e.g.
18. "___ Three Lives"
19. Cheever's "The Sorrows of ___"
23. Work unit
24. ___ von Bismarck
25. What you place around your neck
26. Tint
27. Loos or Ekberg

28. Fall drink
29. Ember
31. Ladies' escorts, for short
32. Speak
33. Kimonos
39. Tout's figures
40. Nabokov novel
41. "That's the story of, that's the ___ love"
44. Jim and Tim
47. Conjunctions
50. Blessed by the rabbi
51. Corned beef seconds
53. Relax, informally
55. TV's Chachi
56. Air

57. Sports fig.
58. Rum cake
59. Ron Howard role
60. Biblical name
61. First fellow
62. ___ silly question . . .
64. Reiner
65. Site of the William Tell legend

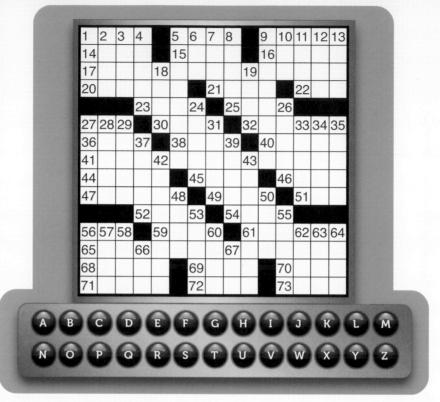

Let's Get Away From It All

Across

1. Bio and chem, e.g.
5. British nobleman
9. Man of morals?
14. Sighed words
15. Medical picture
16. Courageous
17. Early television situation comedy
20. Other than
21. Jealousy
22. Before, poetically
23. Infamous Roman emperor
25. Mt. Rushmore's state: abbr.
27. Sleep state, for short
30. Merit
32. Busybodies
36. Medical school subj.
38. New corp. hires
40. Editor's mark
41. "Get lost!"
44. Dangerous bacteria
45. Scarlett's plantation
46. Skin cream additive
47. Like a high-pitched scream
49. Spinnaker, for one
51. Sun. talk
52. Commoner
54. Shawl or stole
56. Salty expanse
59. "___ to please!"
61. Enchants
65. "Come on, stay a while!"
68. Japanese, perhaps
69. Campus club, commonly
70. Simple melody
71. Leases
72. ___ Fifth Avenue
73. Observes

Down

1. Mall attraction
2. General Mills cereal
3. Apple computer product
4. Lucky number, for some
5. Highway egress

6. Sculpture or dance
7. $10/hour, say
8. French silk center
9. Being temporarily set aside
10. Important time period
11. Use a piggy bank
12. Above
13. Pierre's pop
18. Blunted sword
19. Some briefs, briefly
24. Planet's path
26. Australian eucalyptus eater
27. Rants and raves
28. Methuselah's father
29. Of prime importance
31. Grannies

33. Tough exams
34. Tea type
35. Beef source
37. Bloom associated with Holland
39. Barn floor covering
42. A great deal
43. Salon offerings
48. Bit of foliage
50. Cowardly Lion portrayer
53. Punches
55. Formal agreements
56. Play the lead
57. Abate
58. Similar (to)
60. Pianist Hess
62. Lecher

63. Lion's locks
64. French holy women: abbr.
66. Chow down
67. Acorn's future identity

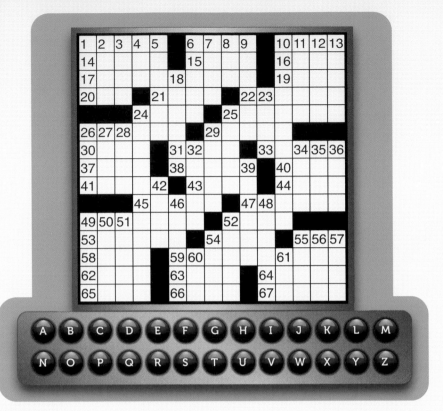

For the Birds

Across

1. Very bitter
6. Pager summons
10. Unwanted e-mail
14. Big zoo animal
15. A, as in Edison
16. Tex-Mex munchie
17. Mean business
19. ___ put it another way
20. Poet's before
21. Means justification, to some
22. Shoveled coal into
24. Some Ivy Leaguers
25. Phrase in many church names
26. Shade of blue
29. Drink greedily
30. "Shake ___!"
31. Auction stipulation
33. Black billiard ball
37. "The ___ McCoys"
38. Kind of guitar in country music
40. Largest Mariana Island
41. Ladies' man
43. Civil Rights activist Parks
44. Fashion magazine
45. Permanent place?
47. Major event in golf
49. Brit's "buddy"
52. Moran of "Happy Days"
53. Like a sponge
54. "Jeopardy!" host Trebek
55. Hellenic H
58. Jacob's hairy brother
59. Humbly admitting error
62. Money for the landlord
63. Pro ___: Lat.
64. Name on jetliners, once
65. Synagogue chests
66. Utters
67. Bad-tempered

Down

1. Comedian Johnson
2. Blacken, as steak
3. Get under one's skin
4. Pen contents
5. "Go on!"

14

6. Poets on heroic themes
7. Members at lodge?
8. Night before Christmas
9. Settles a tab
10. Informer
11. Hooded jacket
12. Put on a show
13. Temperamental
18. Football Hall of Famer Johnny
23. T, on many exams
24. Boys with many badges
25. Desert refuges
26. Singer Vikki
27. Breakfast spread
28. Smile from ear to ear
29. Rest atop

32. Barber's sharpener
34. Swallow eagerly
35. In good health
36. Untouchables, et al.
39. Designer Ralph
42. Pearl Harbor locale
46. Printer parts
48. Oater pistol
49. "Don Giovanni," e.g.
50. Luckless one
51. Didn't pass the bar?
52. Inventor Howe
54. ABA member: abbr.
55. Significant periods
56. "Nothing ___!"
57. Out of kilter

60. Travel org.
61. J.E.B. Stuart's country

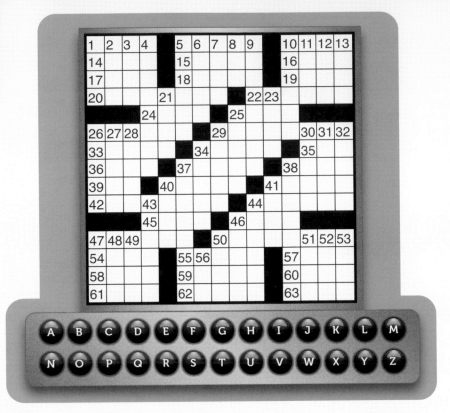

Spin a Web

Across

1. Splashy sound
5. Zoo gift from China
10. Clasp or fastening
14. Adore
15. With the voice
16. Locale
17. Iridescent gemstone
18. Juliet's beau
19. Shopping center
20. Thoroughly cooked
22. Wander widely
24. Created
25. Wise one
26. Like a killer's eyes
29. Flower of the amaryllis family
33. Leads to wolly-doodle
34. Offspring
35. Triumph
36. Object of worship
37. Fry lightly and quickly
38. Color
39. Gentle touch
40. Valley _____
41. Schoolmate with a cap
42. Offensive sights
44. _____ than life
45. Versifier
46. Primary
47. Ghostly apparition
50. Nightly report
54. Ship section
55. Each and all
57. Table spread
58. Rim
59. Bridal path
60. Swear
61. Rip
62. Put off
63. Small mountain lake

Down

1. Do a farm task
2. Swinging stride
3. Egg-shaped
4. In confusion and haste
5. Imitation

6. By one's self

7. Alaskan town

8. Payable

9. Charming and cute

10. Carpenter's tool

11. Spirited horse

12. Wall Street order

13. Pallid

21. Tyne or Tim

23. Matured

25. Connected hotel rooms

26. Petty malice

27. The brink of tomorrow

28. Run away to wed

29. Hoodlums

30. Having debts

31. Then until now

32. Go in

34. Insertion mark

37. Disgruntled person

38. Renegade

40. Twelve inches

41. Platform

43. Spinner of webs

44. Attorney

46. European blackbird

47. Sharpen

48. Traveled on horseback

49. Seaweed

50. Bird's home

51. Thomas _____ Edison

52. Prophet

53. Ripped

56. Compete

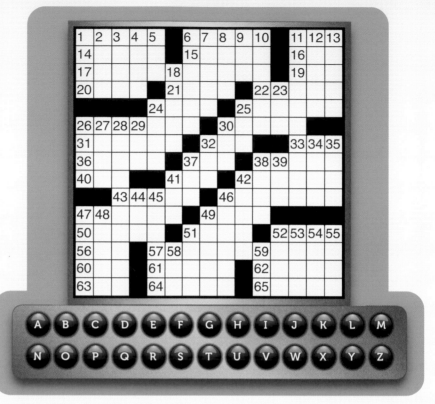

Breakfast's Ready

Across

1. Pursue
6. Oak nut
11. Possessed
14. Surround
15. Recipient
16. Lincoln
17. Breakfast item
19. Me: Fr.
20. Hit in the head
21. Actor Reynolds
22. Sleepy or Doc
24. Emcee
25. Enough
26. Bewitch
30. Collie or poodle, e.g.
31. Confirm
32. Rapture
33. Recede
36. Be
37. Stir
38. Motherless calf
40. Privileges: abbr.
41. Profession
42. Low bubbling sound
43. Sat for the painter
46. Hair
47. Commotion
49. Mardi _____
50. Use
51. _____ Day (Feb. 29)
52. Accountants: abbr.
56. French title of nobility
57. Breakfast item
60. Initials of a classic rock group
61. Not suitable
62. Friendship
63. _____ Francisco
64. Assessments
65. Take it easy

Down

1. Ice cream flavor: abbr.
2. Protagonist
3. "_____ for All Seasons"
4. Piece of plumbing
5. Elizabeth's land: abbr.

6. Adapt
7. Tennis area
8. "Sit _____!"
9. Taping, briefly
10. Tool for a seamstress
11. Breakfast items
12. Scrap a space project
13. Make into a god
18. Black wood
23. Tiny
24. Sword handle
25. Use a crowbar
26. Always
27. Succeeding
28. Breakfast item
29. Towel designation

30. Carton
32. Triangular sail
34. Ill humor
35. Hive dwellers
37. Fashionable, '60s style
38. Membership fees
39. Alternatives
41. Magruder of Watergate
42. Chart
44. Japanese sash
45. Brimstone
46. Pamphlets
47. Hell
48. Part of the soft palate
49. Aladdin's friend
51. Not right

52. Arrive
53. Bucket
54. Dog of literature
55. Underworld river
58. Genetic material: abbr.
59. Pitch

Autumn Delight

Across

1. Rainy day infield cover
5. Part of Batman's getup
9. Jazz musician ___ Calloway
12. Margarine
13. Patron saint of Norway
14. Apple pie ___ mode
15. Natural downside of autumn
18. "Born in the ___," Bruce Springsteen song
19. Lipton product
20. Sibling's daughter
21. Prepare a salad, perhaps
23. Madam's counterpart
24. Sad news item, briefly
26. Forever, seemingly
27. Health club feature
30. Autumn sporting events
34. Ardent devotee
35. Sort
36. Salsa and French Onion, e.g.
37. High or low card
38. Crucifix
40. Like a dishonest deal
43. "Hey, that hurt!"
44. Acquired
47. In autumn, students look forward to this . . . or do they?
50. Lyricist Gershwin
51. Fireplace fodder
52. Data, informally
53. Snoop around
54. Shorten a sentence, maybe
55. "Hey, you!"

Down

1. Vegetarian staple
2. "Ah well"
3. Kinship
4. Vote seeker, briefly
5. Ice cream holders
6. Pond scum
7. Chum
8. Time for a soiree
9. Hangout for bats
10. Actor Guinness
11. Pedestal

16. "___ a girl!"
17. Ventilate
22. Giant Mel of Cooperstown
23. Spain's sun
24. "Keep ___ the Grass"
25. Feathery scarf
26. BPOE member
27. Tiny amounts
28. Vim
29. Beast of burden
31. Eco-friendly transport
32. Ginger ___ (soft drink)
33. Botheration
37. Commercials
38. Perch
39. Barn bird
40. Little cut
41. Munich mister
42. Not home
43. Bear or Berra
45. Dimwits
46. Horse's gait
48. Brick carrier
49. Puppy sound

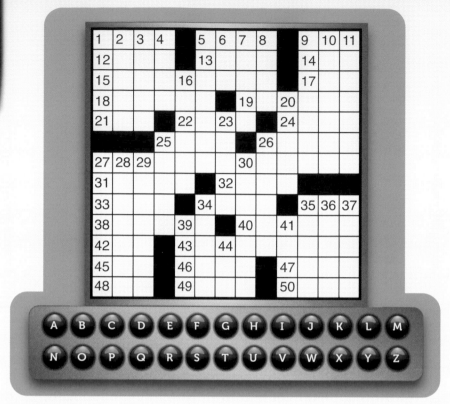

Profit in Baskets

Across

1. Carpenter's holder
5. Satellite receiver
9. Chew the fat
12. Publisher Adolph
13. Black and white sandwich
14. A, in Arles
15. Unconscious state
17. Neither Rep. nor Dem.
18. Abduct
19. More nasty
21. T or F, on exams: abbr.
22. Playground cry
24. ___ noire
25. "The Wizard ___"
26. Irish poet and playwright
27. All profit, in the NBA?
31. Words before "a time"
32. Swiss mountains
33. NY Met, for one
34. Get ready
35. No-goodnik
38. Upper house
40. Danny of "Do the Right Thing"
42. Chiang ___-shek
43. Gift from a bunny
45. Direct ending
46. Land measure
47. Sir's counterpart
48. The, in Berlin
49. Tim of "Sister, Sister"
50. It's figured in square feet

Down

1. Screwdriver ingredient
2. Cause winter isolation
3. Takes off
4. Armchair athlete's channel
5. Miami athlete
6. Rage
7. Terse summons
8. Show optimism
9. Certain African
10. Bening of "American Beauty"
11. Treatment for many illnesses
16. Deemed appropriate
20. Helps during the heist

23. Mystery writers' award
25. Mitchell's Scarlett
26. Modern affluent type
27. Like studded tires
28. Enjoying a furlough
29. More minute
30. Sounded off, like a lamb
34. Type of sign or pipe
35. Like crystal
36. Simple plants
37. Accepted doctrine
39. Pull apart
41. Humorist Bombeck
44. Hindu title

A Matter of Time

Across

1. Ralph of "The Waltons"
6. Chef's meas.
9. Dunderhead
12. Incorporate, as into a city
13. DDT-banning org.
14. Health-care grp.
15. Word after rubber or food
16. Giving more lip
18. Kind of timing
20. Suppresses
22. Cow's comment
23. Union opposition: abbr.
24. Freezing cold
26. Wander
30. Current
34. Color changer
35. Took the gold medal
36. Some plasma screens
37. Gas price-watching org.
40. Beat badly
42. Noon
46. Google is a major one
47. Presses
50. ___ whim
51. Unprocessed
52. Fry in a pan
53. Muddy home
54. Ambulance destinations: abbr.
55. Vote in, as a president

Down

1. "Able ___ I ere I . . . "
2. Uninvited picnic guest
3. On pins and needles
4. Part-time workers
5. Heroic act
6. It may require writing an essay
7. Uncontrollable muscle action
8. A slow stroll, perhaps in Spain
9. Where Dayton is
10. Interjection of agreement
11. Edsel maker
17. Treat with contempt
19. One-twelfth of a foot
20. Iraqi missile
21. "___ with my little eye . . . "

25. Archery bow wood
27. Win a debate
28. Rugged roadsters: abbr.
29. Netting
31. Doctorate hurdle
32. Nighttime flier
33. Not farmed out
38. Burning up
39. Rosy perfume
41. Living on a farm, perhaps
42. The terrible ___
43. Left
44. Cyberspace auction site
45. Conforms strictly
48. Truncation abbreviation
49. Arranged

Explore Your Mind

Across

1. Oil market cartel: abbr.
5. Maker of pens and lighters
8. Use an ax
12. Part of the foot
13. The end of an ___
14. Pushy and unfriendly
15. Leader of the first circumnavigation of the world
17. Prophetic sign
18. Feel poorly
19. Pull on a chain
21. First Spaniard to reach Florida
26. Minor slip
27. "___ River Valley"
28. Temporary bed
30. "Let Us Now Praise Famous Men" writer James
31. Swindle
32. Simple, flowerless plant
33. Part of MPH
34. To's opposite
35. Salute with wine
36. He blazed the Wilderness Road into Kentucky
39. Popular hedging plant
40. Direction on a submarine
41. Economic gain
44. Leader of four expeditions to the New World
49. Old West lawman Wyatt
50. WWW address
51. Basic currency of Italy since 1999
52. Bridge shape
53. Some NFL linemen: abbr.
54. Location of zip code 10001: abbr.

Down

1. Unit of electrical resistance
2. Toy shooter's ammo
3. Brain scan: abbr.
4. Remove stains from
5. Heroine of Disney's "Beauty and the Beast"
6. "Rosemary's Baby" author Levin

7. Military snack bar
8. Oscar winner Russell
9. Drone
10. Poem of praise
11. Write
16. Biting insects
20. Advanced in age
21. Flipped through a book
22. Coloratura's genre
23. Slobber
24. View from the coast
25. Like the Vikings
26. Once around the track
29. High explosive
31. Short hairdo

32. They accompanied Cinderella to the ball
34. Expression of disapproval
35. Vegetarian's protein source
37. Beautiful maiden
38. Snooker targets
41. "Petticoat Junction" star Benaderet
42. Sculling need
43. Tolkien creature
45. Mine output
46. Purchase
47. Coffee dispenser
48. ___ sauce

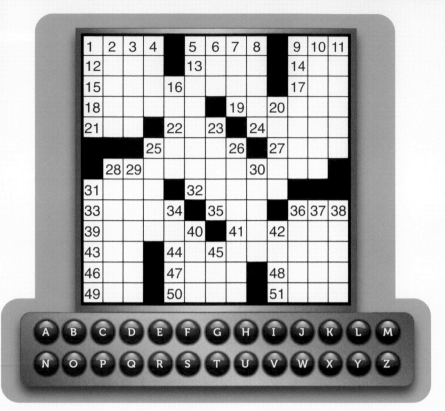

Wax On, Wax Off

Across

1. Former transcontinental planes: abbr.
5. Snoozes
9. ___ Beta Kappa
12. Gumbo vegetable
13. Leave out
14. German article
15. Illegal corn liquor
17. Took a stool
18. Republic in southeast Africa
19. Cauldron
21. Building extension
22. And others: abbr.
24. Not as dark
25. Church structure
27. Proverbial lookalikes
28. Curry favor with
31. Let fall to the floor
32. Show again
33. Plentiful
35. Insecticide banned since 1973
36. X-ray alternative
39. Coral producers
41. Sure winner
43. Singer/actress Zadora
44. Wearing one's birthday suit
46. Show fallibility
47. "Goodbye, Sophia"
48. ___ Royale National Park
49. Object, in law
50. Pack away
51. Prophet

Down

1. French department or river
2. A toast to one's health
3. Wild-haired doll
4. Yemen's capital
5. Pitcher's dream game
6. French friend
7. Variety of champagne
8. Exorbitant, for a price
9. Grinding tools
10. Florida racetrack
11. Buries
16. Just peachy

20. Mammal with a long snout
23. Like a bullfighter
25. Make use of
26. "Antiques ___"
28. Movable cupboard
29. Columnar trees
30. Flexible
31. Well-dressed
34. Many Biblical films
36. Clock climber, in a nursery rhyme
37. Shoulder firearm
38. Suggest
40. State of irritation
42. Japanese sashes
45. Universal ideal

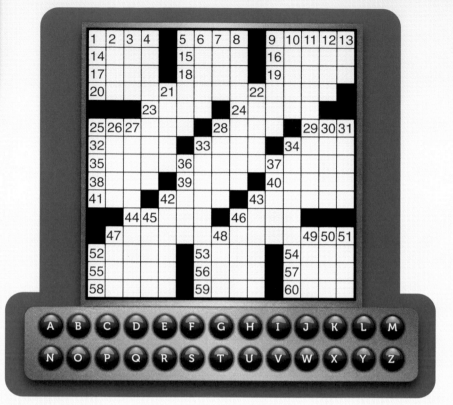

Crossing Caution

Across

1. Bovine baby
5. Shankar of sitar
9. Synagogue official
14. Cain's brother
15. Seuss's "If ___ the Zoo"
16. Kept in the dark
17. Fish in a melt
18. Unsteady gait
19. City near Florence
20. Breaking news order
23. Protrudes
24. Vine-covered
25. Sporty Chevy
28. Sneaker brand
29. New Deal prog.
32. Big name in gas
33. Furnace output
34. Restaurateur Toots
35. "You're one to spout off!"
38. Lodging providers
39. Skin moisturizer
40. Perform better than
41. NFL 3-pointers
42. Type of school
43. Annoy forcefully
44. Caribbean republic
46. Challenging chore
47. Heed advice
52. Titanic-seeker's tool
53. Cry of frustration
54. Boat follower
55. Office worker
56. Cold war defense assn.
57. Former blade brand
58. Soda insert
59. Kind of jacket
60. Wine list datum

Down

1. Rodent exterminators
2. Share a border
3. Jay of TV
4. Pancakes
5. "Sure thing!"
6. Ovine sign
7. Theda Bara role

8. Behind closed doors
9. Putin's land
10. Liqueur flavoring
11. Use all the resources of
12. Waste containers
13. "Give ___ rest"
21. Novelist Scott
22. Madonna musical
25. Ariz. neighbor
26. In the midst of
27. White lightning maker
28. Noted fabulist
30. Polliwogs' places
31. Job-specific vocabulary
33. Golfer's dream
34. Leave stealthily

36. Author Bret
37. At large
42. NASCAR service area
43. Strand on an island
45. Yoga posture
46. Jay Silverheels role
47. Former senator Trent
48. What this isn't
49. Glut
50. It's in a stew
51. Get closer to
52. Draft letters

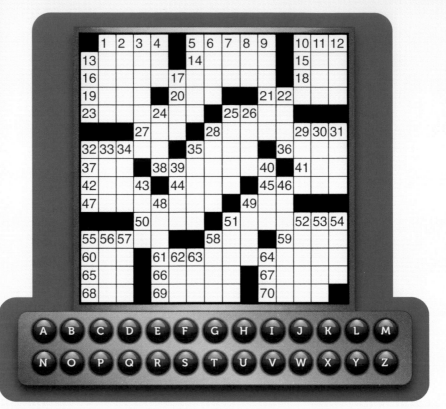

"Easy" Does It

Across

1. "I'm glad that's over!"
5. Censor's sound
10. Not gentile
13. Mae West's invite, in part
14. Superman star
15. Baaed girl
16. Circe and Lorelei
18. Shirt kind
19. Incessantly
20. Excited, with "up"
21. Insignificant sort
23. Misplayed at bridge
25. Worthless?
27. Bishopric
28. Unmatched
32. French seaport
35. 14-Across's role
36. "Death and Fire" artist
37. Potent wriggler
38. Lady Di's family name
41. Mrs.: Fr.
42. "Holy cow!"
44. Oceanbound flier
45. A.K.A. Barnaby Jones
47. Unexpected successes
49. Spelldown
50. Oculist's creation
51. Establishes
55. Pup
58. Game, ___, match
59. SOS
60. "A mouse!"
61. Legendary ballplayer
65. Churchillean gesture
66. Completed
67. Fouled up
68. Chicago trains, for short
69. Rushes
70. Admit, with "up"

Down

1. Annoy
2. Muscle Beach denizens
3. Josephine, e.g.
4. Soppy
5. Poodle or Peke

6. ___ we forget

7. Undergoers of: suf.

8. Garden gal

9. See 1-Down

10. "___ plumerai": Fr.

11. Pitcher

12. Turn on the waterworks

13. Gag or gang ending

17. Name in Korea's history

22. Bubbly bandmaster

24. Understands

25. Mugwump's perch

26. Network

28. William's kin

29. O'Neill's "Desire" site

30. Dotted, coat-of-arms-wise

31. Spotted

32. Entreats

33. Tackle-box item

34. Robert ___

35. Jean and Deborah

39. Hammerhead part

40. "___ pleat," zoot suit feature

43. Former governor and senator Miller

46. Show up

48. Mill contents

49. ___ noire

51. Burpee's wares

52. Lascivious looks

53. "It's nobody ___ business"

54. Drove 80

55. "___ Only Just Begun"

56. Scoundrel

57. Barely makes it

58. Garbo's home: abbr.

62. Compass point

63. Town near Arhem

64. Zebra on the field, for short

Get a Move On

Across

1. Drinking spree
5. Repeat
9. Automobile type
14. Overhang
15. Pal
16. Grassy plain
17. Sonny's ex
18. Part
19. Lubricated
20. Way of life, in the army
23. Automobile
24. Bread soaked in liquid
25. Fit ___ fiddle
27. Ancient Greek promenade
31. Fight against
36. WWII battle sight
38. Killer whale
40. NH city
41. Children's game
44. " . . . partridge in ___ tree"
45. Withered
46. "___ the night before . . . "
47. Minnow
49. Drunkards
51. "You ___ There," hosted by Cronkite
52. Sticky substance
54. Showery month: abbr.
56. Old-fashioned
64. City in upstate New York
65. Periods
66. Roman fiddler
67. River mouth
68. Pinball slip up
69. Cafeteria item
70. Ford flop
71. Only
72. Nick Charles's dog

Down

1. Georgia or Cal
2. Hawaiian isle
3. Outbid, in bridge
4. ___ firma
5. Yellowish brown
6. Sever

7. Hawaiian dance
8. Portents
9. Laggard
10. Lamb pen name
11. Spanish surrealist
12. Dill herb
13. Realm of dreams
21. Units of time: abbr.
22. One of the dwarfs
25. "___ as I'm concerned"
26. Excavate in layers
28. Pull
29. Table scraps
30. Pains
32. Dinner item
33. Flannel sheets, maybe

34. Close at hand
35. Succinct
37. Norse king
39. Sol or space beginning
42. Initial
43. Permit
48. Negative prefix
50. College entrance exam: abbr.
53. U.S. playwright
55. Nina companion
56. Drained
57. Conger and moray
58. Despise
59. Threesome
60. Town ___ meeting
61. This: Sp.

62. Part of Q.E.D.: Lat.
63. Substitute for 32-Down
64. Lyric poem

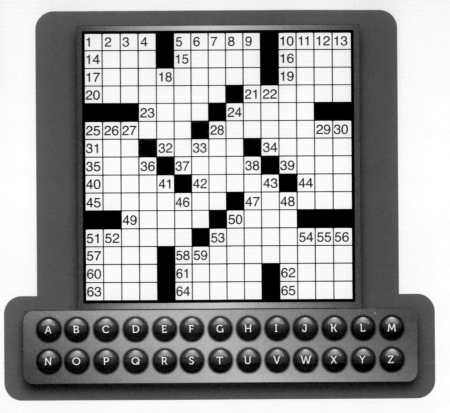

Records

Across

1. Estuaries
5. Brain waves
10. Absent
14. Seven-year problem
15. Goof
16. Miss: Sp. abbr.
17. Record
19. Window part
20. Helix-wise
21. Precisely
23. Baseball's Otis
24. To perfume
25. Described vividly
28. Fondler
31. Poem type
32. Paste-on
34. Move crab-wise
35. VIP's wheels, for short
37. Is intrepid
39. ___ me tangere: Lat.
40. Aerobatic thrills
42. Skewered meal
44. Victory
45. Flowed past
47. Marsh birds
49. Pavlova and Magnani
50. Overstuff
51. Criticized
53. Shook
57. Took the bus
58. Records
60. Burden
61. "In" crowd
62. Beach sight
63. Certain voters: abbr.
64. Mean
65. Featured one

Down

1. Tears
2. "Run ___ the flagpole . . ."
3. Play start
4. WWII navigating system
5. Blew inward
6. Tunes in
7. Catch sight of

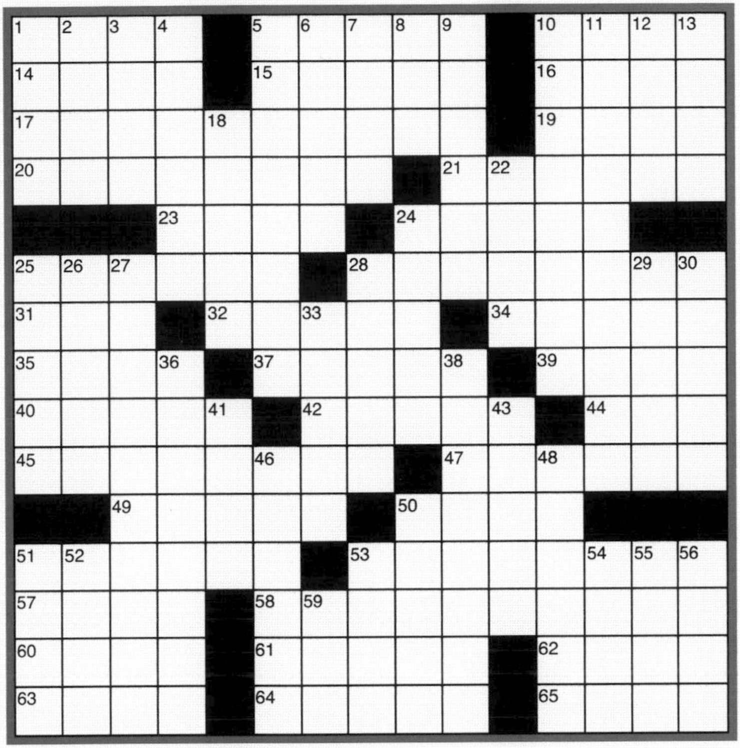

1 2 3 4 5 6 7 8 9 10 11 12 13
14 15 16
17 18 19
20 21 22
23 24
25 26 27 28 29 30
31 32 33 34
35 36 37 38 39
40 41 42 43 44
45 46 47 48
49 50
51 52 53 54 55 56
57 58 59
60 61 62
63 64 65

8. Fruit punch
9. Mail machine
10. Type of bug
11. Records
12. Tamarisk
13. Ivy League campus
18. Cleped
22. Individuals
24. Biblical spy
25. Lounges
26. Mooncalf
27. Written record
28. Concerned
29. Little Eleanor
30. Wagon controls
33. Dessert choices
36. Candor
38. Church area
41. Reasoned
43. Cheer for the diva
46. Lunatic
48. Puts right
50. Thorax
51. Poke
52. Tops
53. Schusses
54. Easy win
55. View from Taormina
56. Forest creature
59. ___ mode

FILE!

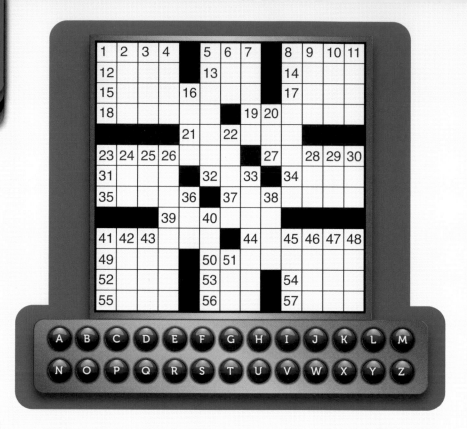

Hurry!

Across

1. Wild guess
5. Mont Blanc, for example
8. Did in
12. Columbus's home
13. Civil War general
14. Scruff
15. "Hurry!"
17. Like
18. One for the books?
19. Facet
21. Frittata
23. Circumspect
27. Small Pacific salmons
31. Aptly named fruit
32. Slow-witted
34. Presidential caucus state
35. Dark-meat choice
37. Bread crumbs, perhaps
39. Like last-minute chores, often
41. Small bar
44. Kind of report
49. First place?
50. "Hurry!"
52. Matador's opponent
53. Sensitive subject, to some
54. Writer Ferber
55. Side order
56. Heir, perhaps
57. 49-Across inhabitant

Down

1. Counter order
2. Friends' pronoun
3. Isn't incorrect?
4. Two out of two
5. Worried, and then some
6. Maui memento
7. Corolla part
8. "Hurry!"
9. Superior, for one
10. Like a De Mille production
11. Left
16. Club choice
20. Dry, as champagne
22. Ruler's decree
23. Kind of instinct

24. "That's disgusting"
25. Baba of "Arabian Nights"
26. "Hurry!"
28. ___ polloi
29. Fess (up)
30. Droop
33. Wet a little
36. Part of H.M.S.
38. Book after John
40. Soft drinks
41. Wagers
42. Superstar
43. Immunizing stuff
45. Word with code or rug
46. Mary Lincoln, née ___
47. Arm bone

48. Bridge coup
51. Pride

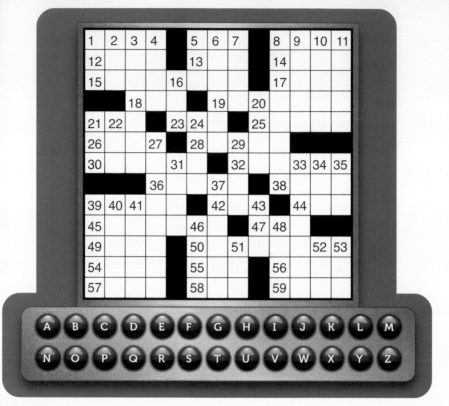

Summertime Fun

Across

1. Give up, as a territory
5. Nautical assent
8. Scottish girl
12. Get-out-of-jail cash
13. Drink like a kitten
14. Director Kazan
15. Summertime warmer
17. Waiter's handout
18. "Gosh!"
19. "On the Road" writer Jack
21. Restaurant bill, informally
23. Wish undone
25. Loosen, as a shoelace
26. Pole or Czech
28. Vintage photograph shade
30. Flower features
32. Make beloved
36. Kitchen gadget
38. Major show, briefly
39. Capital of Jordan
42. It precedes Sept.
44. Teacher's favorite
45. Knitted baby shoes
47. Major ISP
49. Play opener
50. Summertime destination
54. "Scat!"
55. Priest's robe
56. By mouth
57. Merit
58. Put into service
59. Egg layers

Down

1. Cronkite's former employer
2. ___ de Cologne
3. Nutcake
4. "What ___ is new?"
5. "The Greatest" prizefighter
6. Northern Civil War soldier
7. Sporting blade
8. Summertime quaff
9. Native Alaskan
10. Mount in Exodus
11. Spaghetti topper
16. That girl

20. Wreck
21. Cookbook meas.
22. Pub offering
24. Cold War letters
27. Holiday
29. Lima's land
31. Unaccompanied
33. Emulate Christopher Columbus
34. Imitate
35. Deteriorate
37. Portrait painters' stands
39. Humiliate
40. Cocoa-flavored coffee
41. Car engine
43. Car fuel
46. Jacob's twin

48. "Yikes!"
51. Lincoln's nickname
52. Hightailed it
53. Golf legend Ernie

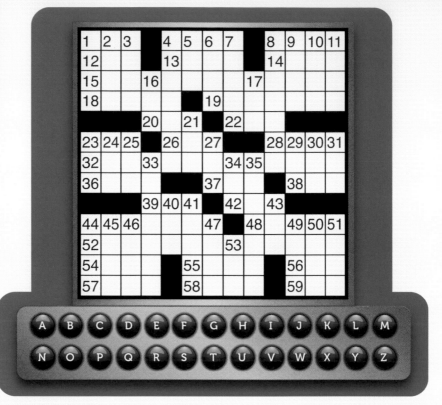

Deli Misadventures

Across

1. Greek letter
4. Raised eyebrow shape
8. "Look what I did!"
12. "You've got mail" co.
13. Hide a treasure, maybe
14. All over again
15. "Were you puzzled over what to buy at the deli?"
18. Clear the windshield
19. Like a docked yacht
20. Sheepish remark?
22. Schuss
23. Somebody special
26. Martinique, par exemple
28. Like a wildly colored tie
32. "How would you describe the deli's decor?"
36. Menial worker
37. Pitcher's stat.
38. British explorer John
39. Participate in an auction
42. Fashion monogram
44. Nudged rudely
48. Chars
52. "And the proprietor? What was he like?"
54. Gait at the track
55. Skin lotion ingredient
56. Beachgoer's quest, often
57. Darns socks, maybe
58. Clucks disapprovingly
59. Wrath

Down

1. Bookie's worry
2. Sewing machine inventor Elias
3. Norwegian saint and king
4. Second first lady's first name
5. Stocking annoyance
6. Grouch
7. Publicizes, slangily
8. Perceptible to touch
9. Cross with a loop
10. Remove from text, briefly
11. Bowled over
16. Weep out loud

17. Vex
21. Everything
23. Big mouth
24. Have bills to pay
25. Tabloid tpc.
27. Give the once-over
29. Anthem contraction
30. Red, white, and blue letters
31. Turn red, perhaps
33. Opens, as a barn door
34. Weep
35. Big bothers
40. ___ Jima
41. Skim, as milk
43. Name of 13 popes
44. Young newts

45. Tackle box item
46. Totally botch
47. Bb. 2-baggers
49. Not pro
50. Paddler's target
51. Word in a New Year's Eve song
53. "All systems go" to NASA

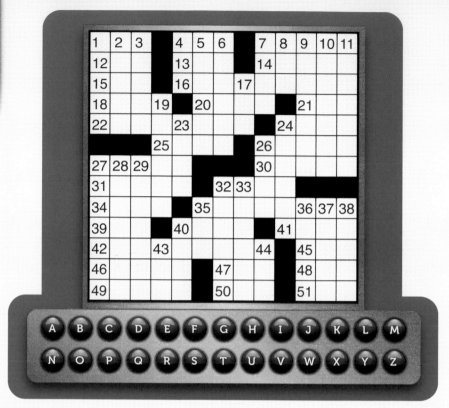

Venomous

Across

1. Messy eater's protection
4. Diet soda from Coca-Cola
7. Movie western
12. Bruce Springsteen's "Born in the ___"
13. In the manner of
14. Temperature taker
15. PC link, for short
16. Invertebrate with stinging tentacles
18. ___ California
20. Wii alternative
21. Formation of flying geese
22. Arthropod with a stinging tail
24. Actress Lollebrigida
25. Parks in front of bus?
26. Religious pamphlet
27. Madras garments
30. Backless slippers
31. Show without a doubt
32. Check the price of, in a way
34. Provide relief
35. Swimmer with a barbed tail
39. Court grp.
40. Head for the heights
41. Roof projection
42. Longest venomous snake
45. Restriction
46. "Delta Dawn" singer Tucker
47. Blockhead
48. Small amount
49. Lunch-time, for some
50. Jargon suffix
51. In poor health

Down

1. Light sources
2. Asimov of science fiction
3. Picked instrument
4. ___ Mahal
5. Joan's role on "Dynasty"
6. Surname of fictional boxer
7. Cameo stone
8. "___ Wiedersehen"
9. Kind of pursuit?
10. Spirit

11. Puts in a microwave, maybe
17. Chaney of horror films
19. Hit the big time
23. Yoga posture
24. Rock genre out of Seattle
26. Secret Service agent, briefly
27. Have a conversation with
28. Graceful horse
29. Country singer Cash
32. Not volatile
33. Thin, wispy cloud type
35. Great Lakes' ___ Canal
36. Hassidic leader
37. Be of use
38. Barbra Streisand film
40. Fraudulent action

43. Swindle
44. Generation

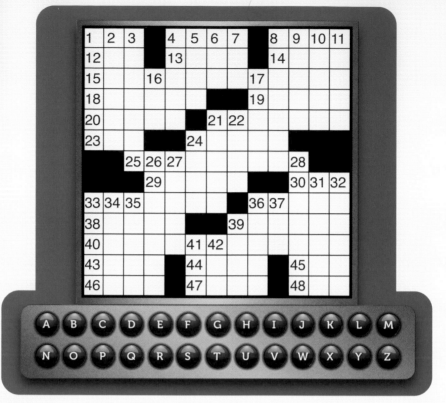

Bad Weather

Across

1. Put into play
4. "___ Blue" (TV show)
8. What a pumpkin grows on
12. Wrinkly dog
13. Honolulu's island
14. Wrinkle remover
15. San Diego Chargers logo
18. Go after
19. "The Big Easy" of golf
20. Drilling site?
21. Ore tester
23. Hosp. trauma units
24. "___ to Avoid" (1965 Herman's Hermits hit)
25. Weather protection at the entrance
29. Tiny amounts
30. Occult ability
33. Female grouse
36. Ipso ___
38. Actor Davis
39. Suit maker
40. Suddenly astonished
43. "When you get right down ___ . . . "
44. Beef or pork
45. Location of UFO sightings
46. Sgt. Snorkel's dog
47. Nimble
48. Road twist

Down

1. Missing one's bedtime
2. One seeking a mate
3. Picnic contest
4. Tally mark
5. Pull quickly
6. Fraternity letter
7. Pester for payment
8. Violinist's asset
9. Subtle sarcasm
10. "It's the truth!"
11. Participate in
16. Cap
17. Painting surface
21. Jordan's capital
22. Brewskis

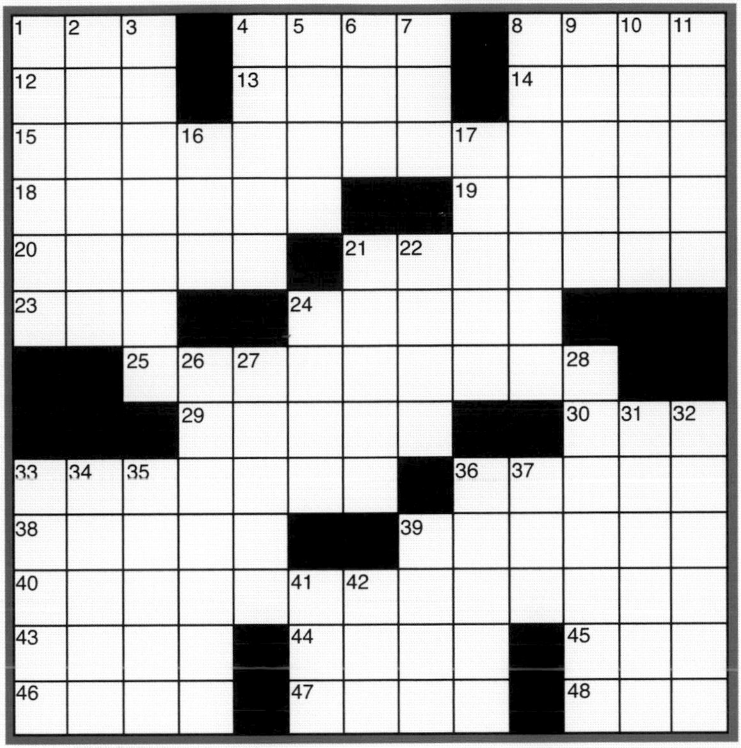

24. Comedian Johnson
26. Connect with
27. Partner of aahed
28. Howard Hughes became one
31. Part of a mutual fund
32. 1982 comedy about high schoolers
33. ___ voce
34. ___ in the dark
35. Astronaut's attire
36. Silent film comedian Arbuckle
37. Tire filler
39. Ruler mixed up in arts?
41. In typography-speak, more than one long dash
42. Account exec

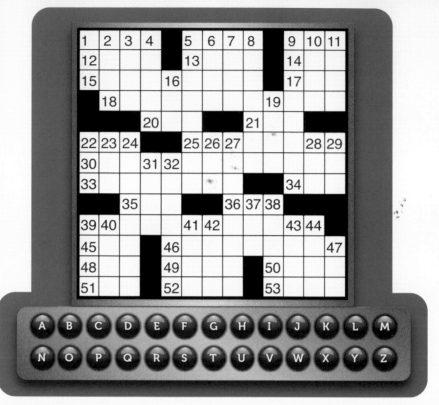

Horsing Around

Across

1. Cambodian's neighbor
5. Communist island
9. Lotus programs co.
12. ___ sod
13. Mimicked
14. Miss Piggy's pronoun
15. Taken the place of
17. It has a small head
18. Forget a horse?
20. Radiation protection no.
21. Some batters: abbr.
22. Trumpet location
25. In a state of joy
30. Way to a dark horse?
33. Not type A
34. Former White House resident's inits.
35. Bumbling bloke
36. PD notice
39. Lighter version of the iron horse?
45. To write quickly
46. Gingham dog fighter
48. Hail
49. Coast-to-coast highway
50. Not a one
51. Color of Santa's suit
52. Fashion designer Cassini
53. They, in Italian

Down

1. Keep the rhythm, perhaps
2. Chuck
3. Ship's safe side
4. Innovation beginnings
5. 1962 movie thriller remade in 1991
6. Doing
7. "Where have you ___?"
8. Increased
9. Identity thief
10. One way to cook cabbage
11. Tea flavorer
16. Winner of the Hart Trophy in the NHL
19. Arctic fish

22. List-ending abbr.
23. Melodramatic cry
24. Sent in another direction
26. B followers
27. Pretty mad
28. Descartes' conclusion
29. Nancy Grace's employer
31. Paper quantity
32. Ex ___ (by virtue of position)
37. Army rank: abbr.
38. Hard stuff
39. Between open and closed
40. Nothing, in a set
41. Abbr. in many U.S. org. names
42. 1997 Peter Fonda title role
43. Key cards in 21

44. "___ and the Real Girl" (2007 movie)
47. Head opposite

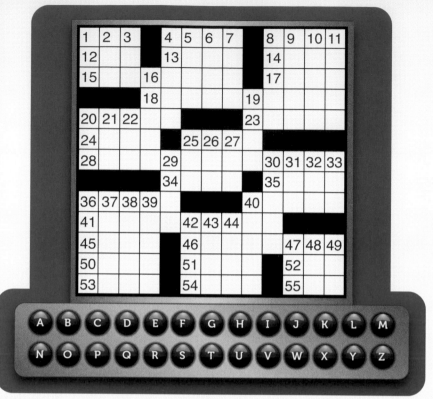

Dairy Folk

Across

1. Audi competitor
4. In a crowd of
8. Juicy fruit
12. Item worn around the neck
13. Baked southern dish
14. Tops
15. Sushi bar staple
17. Cause to wince
18. Timid folk
20. Intoxicate
23. Snap course
24. One of Shakespeare's villains
25. Inspiration source
28. Clumsy folk
34. "Love Makes the World Go Round" singer Jackson
35. Brigham Young's home
36. Dwight's opponent in '52 and '56
40. Acting profession
41. Ineffectual folk
45. Temple's first husband
46. Where grapes grow
50. Wrestling style
51. One of the Great Lakes
52. F or G, but not H
53. Straddle
54. First cops in the USA
55. Feller in the woods

Down

1. Hardly the big shot
2. Dairy sound
3. The Appian ___
4. Distinguished (from)
5. Pained expression
6. Ancient Machu Picchu dweller
7. Consider
8. ___ New Guinea
9. Goofs off
10. Make whole
11. The brainy bunch
16. Run quickly
19. Hammer feature
20. Lobster-eater's attire

21. It's found dans le bain
22. "___ Bilko," Steve Martin film
25. Soldier's fare, for short
26. Mystery flyer
27. Pride, lust, or envy
29. Amend text
30. Full of determination
31. Terminal posting: abbr.
32. Kind of doll
33. The queen as a subject?
36. Hoard
37. Root out
38. Long-necked animal
39. Ohio's "City of Invention"
40. Trusty mount

42. Dutch ___
43. Gossamer
44. Take a short cut?
47. Rap sheet letters
48. Carnivorous dinosaur name
49. Hair colorer

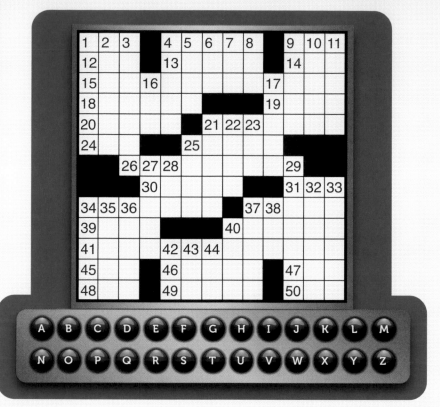

Pitching Records

Across

1. "2001: A Space Odyssey" computer
4. Poisonous substance
9. Boxer's target
12. Yes, in Paris
13. Like a good guard
14. Freud focus
15. Pitcher with most consecutive scoreless innings (59)
18. Cowboy competitions
19. Cowboy's bed
20. Crawled out of bed
21. Reluctantly abstains from
24. Go off course
25. "Forget it!"
26. Pitcher with most career no-hitters (7)
30. Dress to the ___
31. List maker's space saver
34. Stooge
37. Language of Sri Lanka
39. Theatrical award
40. League of Nations home
41. Pitcher with most career shutouts (110)
45. Summer in Le Havre
46. Vacate
47. Type
48. Like a boiled lobster
49. Specialty
50. Maggie, to Lisa, briefly

Down

1. "Yippee!"
2. Roman goddess of dawn
3. Command to a dog
4. Nevada resort
5. Spanish cheers
6. Gen-___ (baby boomer's successor)
7. Kind of agent
8. Number in a series
9. He was affiliated with Peter, Paul, and Mary
10. Broker
11. Does the trick

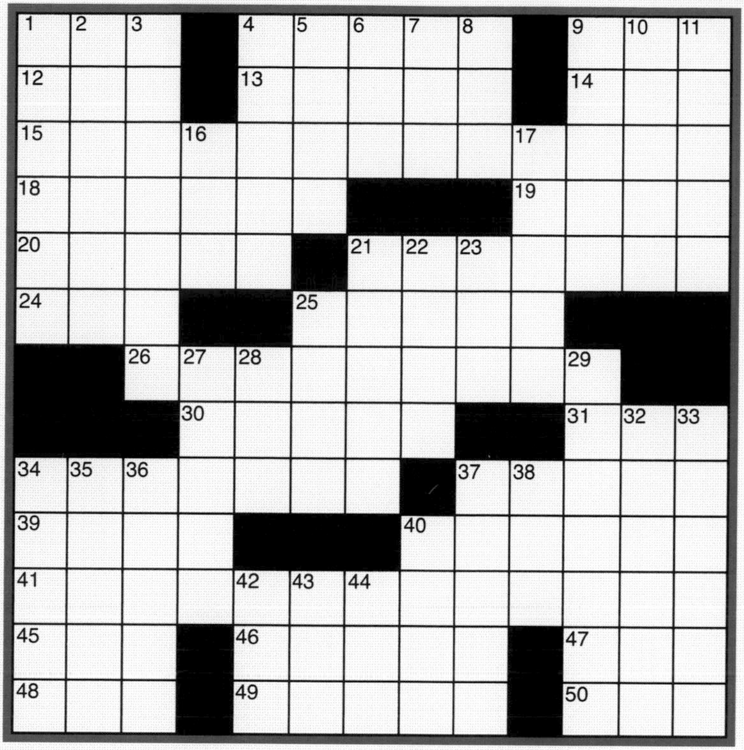

16. Band leader Brown
17. Spanish vacation island
21. Continue a subscription
22. Makes a mistake
23. Dirty digs
25. Grandma's nickname
27. Start
28. Sass
29. Mortal enemy
32. Copenhagen's ___Gardens
33. Chain sounds
34. Cringe
35. Diminish
36. Like a bathroom floor
37. Snicker
38. Abby's sister
40. Poli-sci subj.
42. Reindeer feeder?
43. Old car
44. Pickle container

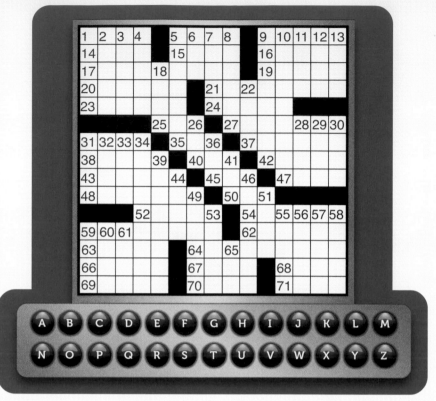

Awfully Nice

Across

1. Korea's continent
5. Napoleon's isle of exile
9. Wedding party transports
14. Shellac ingredients
15. Refrigerate
16. "___ a Parade"
17. Fill-in for a talk show, e.g.
19. Chimney channels
20. Dress, as a judge
21. "Ditto"
23. Imp
24. Got up
25. Decompose
27. London cathedral
31. Mexican money
35. Forty winks
37. Bisects
38. Strong glue
40. Teacher's favorite
42. Explosive experiment, for short
43. Colored anew
45. Hit with a stun gun
47. Panamas and boaters
48. Joins forces (with)
50. Practical joke
52. "___ mio!"
54. Search parties, in the Old West
59. Retaliation
62. Geritol target
63. Mistake
64. "Heavens!"
66. Skirt style
67. Until
68. "I cannot tell ___"
69. Singer/actress Della
70. Fair hiring org.
71. Bigwigs in biz

Down

1. Horatio of inspirational books
2. Spa spot
3. Bakery employees
4. Org.
5. Level of authority
6. Toilet, in London

7. "Blame it on the ___ Nova"
8. Sanctuary centerpieces
9. Threescore and ten, maybe
10. Sickness
11. Pout
12. Finished
13. Ousted Zaire ruler Mobuto ___ Seko
18. Way up the ski slope
22. Wool-eating insect
26. Faucet
28. Middle layer of the eye
29. "___ we forget"
30. Grounded sound breakers: abbr.
31. Saucy, as a young lass

32. Pointless fencing sword
33. Fountain treat
34. What 17-Across, 64-Across, 10-Down, and this puzzle's title are
36. Dispenser candy
39. "You betcha!"
41. "You're it!" chasing game
44. Performing twosomes
46. One time Haitian dictator, informally
49. One of ten in Exodus
51. Bell hit with a hammer
53. Wed on the run
55. Glacial ridge
56. Photographer's request
57. Old MacDonald's refrain

58. Bank vaults
59. Back side
60. ___ Stanley Gardner
61. ___-dieu (prayer bench)
65. Oklahoma Native American

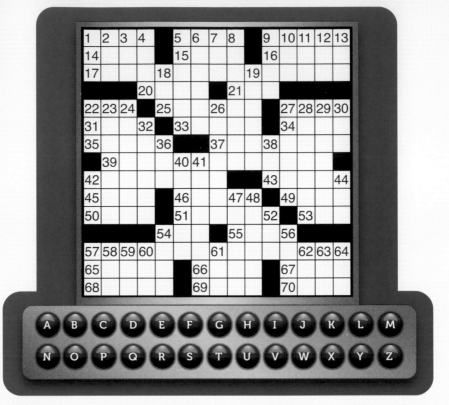

Carrying On

Across

1. Ring
5. Mardi _____
9. Do a Thanksgiving dinner job
14. Bear constellation
15. River past Buckingham
16. Foreign
17. Competitions with forwards and guards
20. SASE, e.g.
21. "For shame!"
22. Cookie-selling org.
25. "Tommy" rock opera group
27. "I _____ Little Prayer for You"
31. Holler
33. Quite pale
34. Retired prof's title: abbr.
35. Actress Normand of the silents
37. Brunch time, maybe
39. Saint Patrick's Day parade participant, likely
42. Provided funds for, as a car loan
43. Facial features
45. _____ the Red
46. China's Zhou _____
49. Alternative magazine founded in 1984
50. 6/6/44
51. The highest volcano in Eur.
53. Gridiron gains: abbr.
54. Poetic meadow
55. Gambler's figures
57. Facially expressing disapproval, perhaps
65. Small musical combos
66. "The Virginian" author Wister
67. State settled by Brigham Young
68. Apprehension
69. Tree house?
70. Like many a horror film

Down

1. Place to get a Guinness

2. Memorable period
3. Ninny
4. Fresh body of water
5. "Aha!"
6. Russian coins
7. Botanist Gray
8. Bookstore section
9. Parakeet's place
10. _____ carte
11. Edge
12. Neck with a point
13. Coast Guard rank: abbr.
18. Treebeard in "The Lord of the Rings," e.g.
19. Big name in model trains
22. Phys. ed. class locale
23. Gull or tern
24. Tirane's country
26. Cajole
27. "Ciao!"
28. General pardon
29. Accountant's closing time
30. Hand and shoulder connector
32. Inheritance
36. Hospital staffer: abbr.
38. Moving vehicle
40. Bygone block deliverers
41. It has five sides
42. Gave sustenance
44. French possessive pronoun
47. Observes Yom Kippur
48. Tab key function
52. Commercials
54. It might be headed "To Do"
56. Fake vending machine coin
57. School group: abbr.
58. Big coffee server
59. 18-wheeler
60. "Mayday!"
61. Be in arrears
62. "How was _____ know?"
63. Golfer's standard
64. Timid

About Face

Across

1. Intended course
5. Leaf of grass
10. Practice boxing
14. No friend to Othello
15. Hammerin' Hank
16. Superman's childhood pal Lang
17. Bancroft–MacLaine film
20. In order
21. Be in accord
22. Cravats
23. Market places in ancient Rome
25. Riding clothes
28. Exacts
31. South Seas romance of 1847
32. Greased
33. Narrow inlet
35. Novel by John Marquand
39. Spring collectors: abbr.
40. Eroded
41. "Planet of the _____"
42. Calmed with medication
44. Ancient Palestinian fortress
46. Organization: abbr.
47. Sing with great force
48. Look fixedly
51. Snakes
55. Lets the heat in
58. Poker stake
59. Of space
60. Speedy animal
61. Film holder
62. "Funny Girl" Brice
63. Sea eagle

Down

1. Bread used in the East
2. The Cowardly Lion actor
3. Land in Caesar's day
4. Memo
5. Flat-bottomed boats
6. Bowling alleys
7. Parched
8. Knotts
9. School subject: abbr.
10. "I Like Ike," e.g.

11. Two of a kind
12. Bancroft or Boleyn
13. Evaluate
18. Part of a military group
19. Thanksgiving Day event
23. Wrongdoer
24. Hebrew measure
25. Mesa dwellers
26. Cupids in paintings
27. Capital of Idaho
28. Broke bread
29. Mountain dweller of Tibet
30. Begot
32. Many times
34. Handle: Lat.
36. Raises the nap

37. Fare for Dobbin
38. "_____ luxury of woe"
    (Thomas Moore)
43. Type of grass
44. Just
45. Paradise for skiers
47. Irish playwright
48. Play the lead
49. Choreographer Tommy
50. Comedian Johnson
51. British carbine
52. At hand
53. Mountain lake
54. Pintail duck
56. Blockhead
57. Gun owners group: abbr.

Treed

Across

1. Foot in verse
5. Glades
10. Murray and West
14. Bar follower
15. "Middlemarch" author
16. Jerez jar
17. Handle, for Horace
18. Lobo
20. Prescribed amounts
22. Balzac's "Le _____ Goriot"
23. Woods's prop
24. Pert lass
26. Gallaudet beneficiary
28. Unmarried male
32. Pumice
36. Seraglios
37. Chemical ending
38. Inclination
39. Muralist José Maria
40. Gambled
43. Drat!
44. Athenian demagogue
46. Cicero's "Where?"
47. Rational
48. Minor Persian despot
50. Bridged
52. Dutch export
54. Conservative: abbr.
55. Southern state: abbr.
58. Part of a geom. sign-off
60. Old magistrates
64. Exponents in higher math
67. Fast time
68. "Jeopardy!" host, to friends
69. Caravansary
70. Freeway portion
71. Created
72. Time periods
73. Fillip

Down

1. Hussein's former land
2. Japanese aborigine
3. "Wild Horse _____" (Grey)
4. Mercantile subsidiary
5. Assigned

6. Samuel's counselor
7. Flaccid
8. Like oak leaves
9. Metrical measures
10. Cut grass
11. "Thanks _____"
12. She: Fr.
13. Ump's call
19. Respond
21. "_____ Kiss": Rodin
25. Morrison, of literature
27. Old Wimbledon rival
28. Autumn pears
29. Miss St. John
30. Editor's mark
31. Like some gems

33. Stately
34. Jejune
35. Used an abacus
41. Zaragoza's river
42. Diacritical mark
45. Consumer advocate
49. Congregation
51. Norm: abbr.
53. San _____, CA
55. Hoax
56. Manilow's girl of song
57. Matured
59. N.Y. type way
61. Spare
62. Sicilian resort
63. Word with child or ladder

65. Bunyan's tool
66. Cover with graffiti

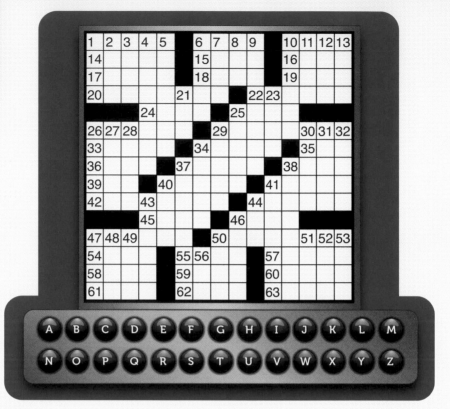

Panagram

Across

1. Is apparently
6. Teen's "Yeah, right!"
10. Apparel
14. ". . . who ___ heaven"
15. Swiss hero William
16. Skin moisturizer
17. Proof of car ownership
18. Ward of "Sisters"
19. Techie workplaces, often
20. Applied pressure to
22. Moon stages
24. Length times width
25. Comet alternative
26. Barely burned
29. Animal with a duck bill
33. Shout of encouragement
34. Streisand's "Funny Girl" role
35. One ___ million
36. Tattered attire
37. Disreputable doctor
38. Move like a hummingbird
39. Fruit-drink suffix
40. "I Remember Mama" actress Irene
41. Plundered treasure
42. Nonconformist
44. Intermediate weight boxer, for short
45. Corleone's creator
46. Notorious pirate captain
47. Wings it
50. Alluded to
54. Swamp reptile, for short
55. Burglar's take
57. Tater state
58. Simba's love, in "The Lion King"
59. Hershiser of baseball
60. Wrapped movie monster
61. Series ending
62. Money rolls
63. Fencing blades

Down

1. Brief entrance exams
2. "ER" actor La Salle

3. Words to Brutus
4. Odometer readings
5. Scoffing sort
6. Totally befuddled
7. Sunflower edible
8. Not in the pink
9. Pancake
10. Large collection of stars
11. Wistful word
12. Dressing gown
13. Porgy's lady
21. Last letter, in Britain
23. Despise
25. Wonderland visitor
26. "Beat it!"

27. "If ___ nickel for every time . . . "
28. Israeli desert
29. Shenanigan
30. Light in the furnace
31. Link up
32. Mythical reveler
34. Con game
37. "The $64,000 Question," e.g.
38. Went out of business
40. Defeat decisively
41. "Nighty-night" hour
43. Grand in scope
44. Finish first
46. Stops, as a story
47. Teen outbreak

48. Doggone!
49. Whatever she wants, she gets
50. Shaded
51. Title for Judi Dench
52. Sigh words
53. Playthings
56. Coach Parseghian of Notre Dame fame

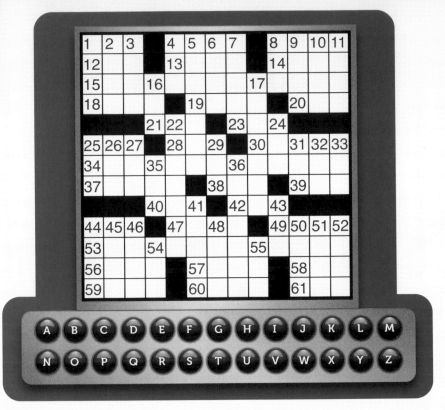

Winter Wonders

Across

1. "It ___ a very good year"
4. Resistance units
8. Rich topsoil
12. Picnic pest
13. Gather, as grain
14. Otherwise
15. Fun winter "battle"
18. Mama's mate
19. Letter opener?
20. Sailor's assent
21. "Hee ___"
23. Gratuity
25. Chicken ___ king
28. Service station purchase
30. Big faux pas
34. Athletes on the ice
37. Durable alloy
38. Nevertheless
39. It's over an I
40. Precious stone
42. "...___ the land of the free..."
44. Airport abbr.
47. Suds maker
49. Your mom's sister
53. In some houses, this is a winter tradition
56. Agitate
57. Beginner
58. Fed. property overseer
59. River to the Caspian Sea
60. Auto pioneer Ransom Eli
61. Kind of curve

Down

1. Bee's cousin
2. "___ and the King of Siam"
3. "Cut it out!"
4. Spherical body
5. Progress
6. Like about half of us
7. Water balloon sound
8. Oahu garland
9. Olympic gymnast Korbut
10. Pasty-faced
11. Parcel (out)

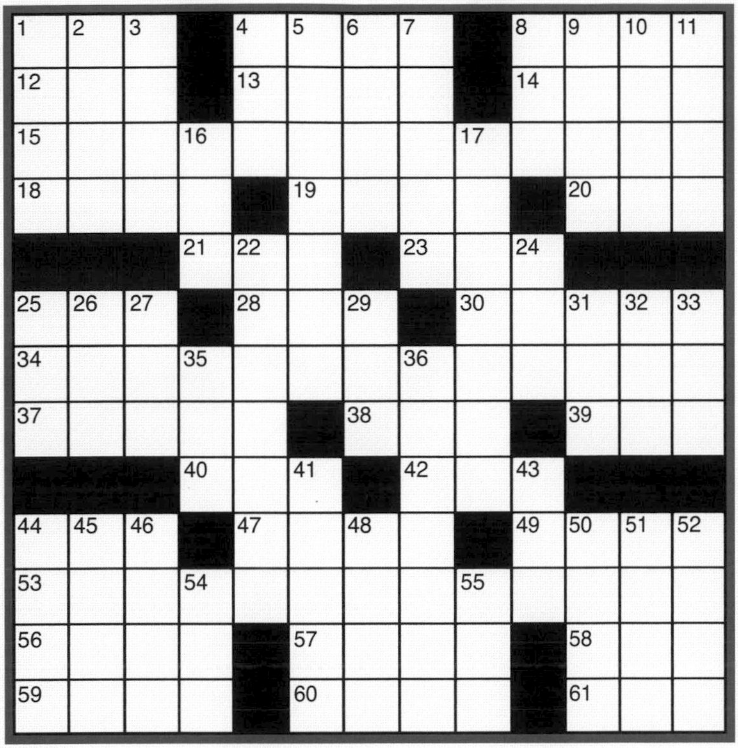

16. Baby's bawl
17. Warship
22. Eternal
24. Settle, as a debt
25. Contented sighs
26. Fate
27. Sharpshooter
29. Mata Hari, for example
31. Provided with sustenance
32. To and ___
33. Winter hrs. in Boston
35. Beer barrel
36. Large, spotted cat
41. Phrase on a coat of arms
43. Pied Piper follower
44. Hosiery shade
45. Norse god of thunder
46. Diva's big song
48. ___ nitrate
50. Egg on
51. Loch of note
52. Afternoon socials
54. Under the weather
55. "Mayday!"

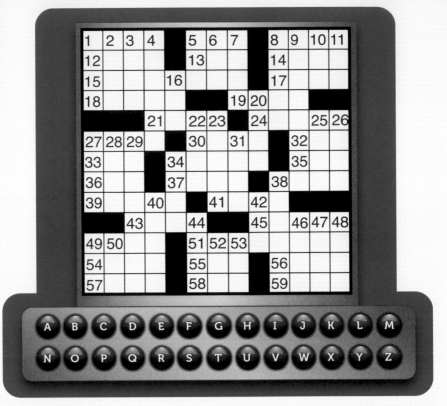

Spring Has Sprung!

Across

1. Barbecue fare
5. Swelled head
8. Pound the keyboard
12. Not quite round
13. Like sushi dishes
14. Horse color
15. In spring, this sport goes into training
17. "___ Lang Syne"
18. Follow
19. Twirl
21. Golf gadgets
24. Michael, Gabriel, or Raphael
27. Foot part
30. Poor box offerings
32. China's Chairman ___
33. Zero
34. Forest units
35. Perissodactyl mammal
36. Foot digit
37. Ersatz butter
38. Chip in chips
39. Ringo the drummer
41. Baby branch
43. Zero
45. Gymnast Comaneci
49. Etcher's fluid
51. In spring, this is a farmer's chore
54. Solo
55. 007-creator Fleming
56. Despise
57. Corporate symbol
58. IRS 1040 pro
59. Soothing plant

Down

1. Judge's garb
2. "The Terrible" czar
3. Lowest male singing voice
4. Detective
5. Important time period
6. Guy's date
7. Nocturnal hooters
8. Railroad vehicle
9. In spring, his fancy turns to love

10. Buddy
11. Terminate
16. Hive dweller
20. ". . . do not ___ Go, do not collect . . . "
22. "My Name Is ___" (TV show)
23. Icy rain
25. Whence the sun rises
26. Be an also-ran
27. Industrious insects
28. Civil insurrection
29. In spring, a big task
31. Catty remark?
34. Ripped
38. Christie of mysteries

40. Cowboy show
42. Traveler's haven
44. Saga
46. Old telephone feature
47. Division word
48. "The African Queen" screenwriter James
49. The whole shebang
50. What lovebirds do
52. Place for a grandchild, maybe
53. Santa ___ winds

Fruit Salad

Across

1. Rivers of comedy
5. Collect
10. Tabloid mention
14. Exile isle
15. Programming language
16. Writer/director Ephron
17. Larynx part
19. Publicist's concern
20. Certain Asian American
21. "My boy. . . "
22. Word in old matrimonial rites
23. Lady dealing in futures?
26. 1965 march site
28. Pry
30. Browning work
33. Mule of song
36. Exodus figure
38. Baby grand, perhaps?
39. Old TV's "___ Three Lives"
41. Kind of code
43. Quotation notation
44. Half of 1960s quartet
46. Reporter's coup
48. Bass, for one
49. Cue
51. Inbox contents
53. ___ Ark
55. Deadlock
59. Soapstone component
61. "Boola-Boola" singer
63. Ties up
64. Airline since 1948
65. Midday appointments, maybe
68. Actor Rob of "Masquerade"
69. Gates licensed it to IBM in 1981
70. Vaquero's weapon
71. Not as much
72. Gives ___ (cares)
73. Sole

Down

1. Denims
2. Nostalgic number
3. Humiliate
4. Stoolies, sometimes

Crossword Grid

Grid with numbered cells: 1, 2, 3, 4, 5, 6, 7, 8, 9, 10, 11, 12, 13 (top row); 14, 15, 16; 17, 18, 19; 20, 21, 22; 23, 24, 25, 26, 27; 28, 29, 30, 31, 32; 33, 34, 35, 36, 37, 38; 39, 40, 41, 42, 43; 44, 45, 46, 47, 48; 49, 50, 51, 52; 53, 54, 55, 56, 57, 58; 59, 60, 61, 62, 63; 64, 65, 66, 67; 68, 69, 70; 71, 72, 73.

5. Lawyers' org.

6. It'll give you a sense of direction

7. They're filled with venom

8. Missile shelters

9. Play parts

10. Sleepless state

11. Project head

12. Pennsylvania port

13. Lots of

18. Saint Catherine's hometown

24. Ivory bar?

25. Wounds

27. An arborist might do it

29. ___ de Leon

31. Organic compound

32. Pitch

33. Fool

34. Winged

35. Vehicle buyers' protection

37. "Whither thou goest" addressee

40. Ancient Greek associated with a sword

42. Good earth

45. Upscale bath feature

47. Spoke (up)

50. Louise's film friend

52. Certain washbowl

54. Sloppy snow

56. Saint Elizabeth Ann ___

57. Fishhook line

58. English class assignment

59. Relate

60. African succulent

62. ___-European

66. Emulate a pigeon

67. Marshall Plan implementer's monogram

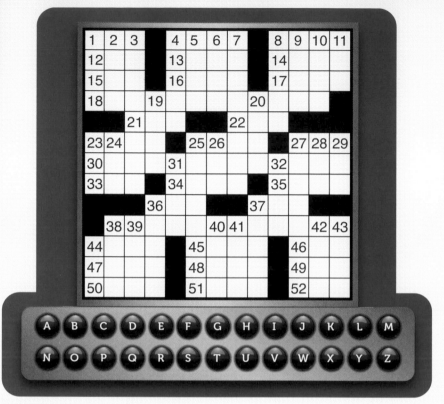

Colorful Clues

Across

1. What Wednesday's child is full of
4. TV comedian Carey
8. Jupiter has a big red one
12. Shanty
13. Solemn vow
14. Last item in Pandora's box
15. First person in Germany
16. Tubular pasta
17. Cajun thickener
18. Yellow Book listings
21. Quasimodo portrayer Chaney
22. Bear's foot
23. Comic book cry of pain
25. Skater's jump
27. South Korean automaker
30. Little black book listings
33. Pig shelter
34. Elbows in pipe
35. Not so much
36. Metro maker
37. Matador's support
38. Blue book listing
44. Small songbird
45. Female friend in France
46. Poison ____
47. Words of comparison
48. It's south of Ken.
49. Born
50. Stellar org.
51. Football positions
52. Word after natural or tear

Down

1. Party line enforcer
2. Cry of pain
3. Study of behavior
4. Typical roses order
5. Gutter filler
6. "____, Brute?"
7. Cries softly
8. She needed taming, according to Shakespeare
9. Start of Ben Franklin's almanac?

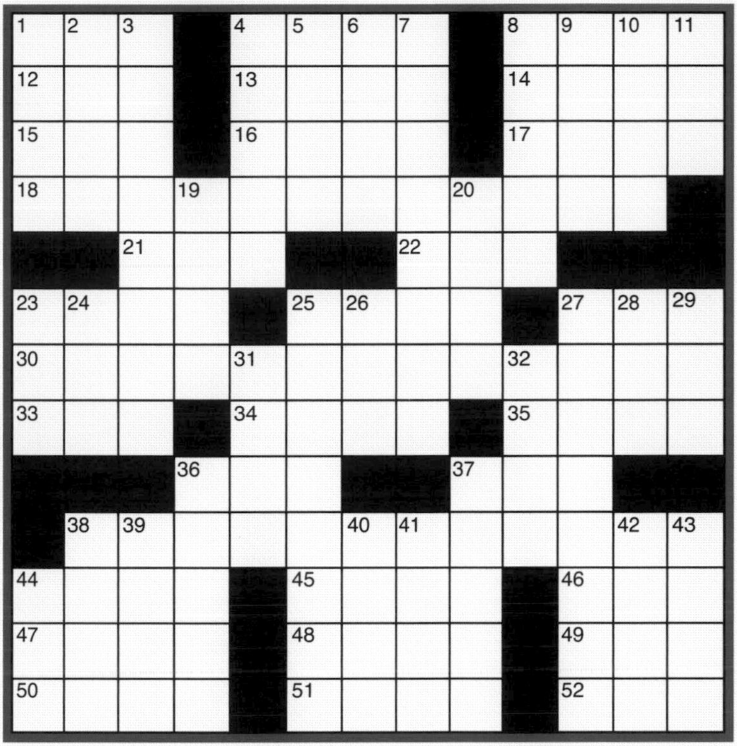

The crossword grid:

1	2	3	■	4	5	6	7	■	8	9	10	11
12			■	13				■	14			
15			■	16				■	17			
18			19					20				■
■		21			■		22				■	■
23	24			■	25	26		■		27	28	29
30			31					32				
33		■	34			■		35				
■		36			■		37			■	■	
■	38	39			■	40	41			42	43	
44				■	45		■		46			
47				■	48		■		49			
50				■	51		■		52			

10. ____ Dei
11. Cowboy nickname
19. Start of a bedtime prayer
20. Indonesian island
23. "You are correct, sir!"
24. Phone line: abbr.
25. Distribute according to plan
26. Org. that played for one season in 2001
27. Position of prayer
28. Driver's license and the like abbr.
29. Beast of burden
31. "Walk on the Wild Side" singer Lou
32. Jazz singer Fitzgerald
36. Birthplace of Italian poet Eugenio Montale
37. Kilns
38. Twinkling bear
39. Drops below the horizon
40. The last word in churches?
41. Cacao pod covering
42. Layer of the iris
43. They may be peeled
44. Victory

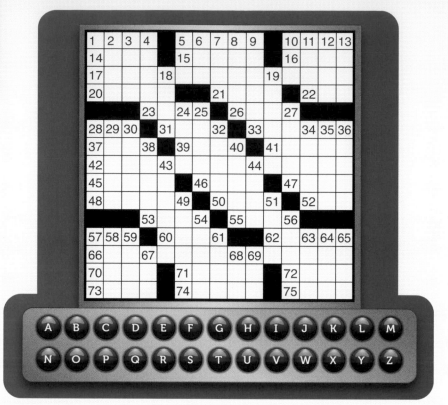

Playing Post Office

Across

1. Wine barrel
5. Gold-related
10. Inevitable destruction
14. Comrade in arms
15. Spanish silver
16. Aptly named tropical fruit
17. Language not used in polite society
20. Spooky
21. Asian nursemaid
22. Contractor's quote: abbr.
23. Omelet ingredients
26. Put one's foot down?
28. Dashboard meas.
31. Fireworks reactions
33. Peaceful
37. ___ the Red
39. Spinning toys
41. Districted
42. Exceed accepted limits
45. Be crazy about
46. Plumlike gin flavoring
47. Distinctive flair
48. Desired answer to "Are you going to help me?"
50. Lane of the "Daily Planet"
52. Capone and Gore
53. Garbage barge
55. Implore
57. School of thought: suf.
60. River to the Caspian Sea
62. Gather up
66. Official okay
70. Winter Olympics sledding event
71. Mexican mister
72. Infamous Roman emperor
73. Shorten text, perhaps
74. Clear the chalkboard
75. Grasp firmly

Down

1. Sidewalk eatery
2. Skin cream additive
3. Insulting remark
4. ___ eleison ("Lord, have mercy")

5. Gorilla, for one

6. Final: abbr.

7. Pro ___

8. Tabloid twosomes

9. Gem units

10. Close pair

11. Monster

12. Auto pioneer Ransom Eli

13. Spray

18. Toy block brand

19. Breathe laboriously

24. Fourth-century invader

25. Loafers and oxfords

27. Laboring class member

28. Satisfy, as a loan

29. Priggish one

30. Japanese soup flavorings

32. Compete in a bee

34. Bomber ___ Gay

35. Katmandu's land

36. Ideal places

38. Evert of tennis

40. Nosy one

43. It sits in a saucer

44. Bride's head covering

49. In a glum mood

51. Scorch

54. Small thin cookie

56. Surrounded by

57. ___ of Wight

58. Type of poker game

59. Crèche figures

61. Turner the actress

63. Allege

64. Garment for a rani

65. Pig's dinner

67. Was introduced to

68. Not neg.

69. Opposite of post

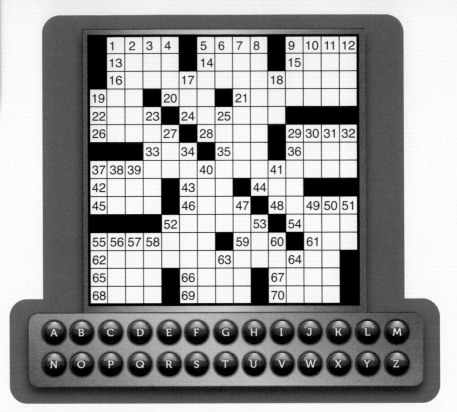

International Headlines

Across

1. Writing tablets
5. Stylish
9. Excellent: sl.
13. Sad news item
14. Gossipy Barrett
15. Plumb crazy
16. Angry Emerald Isle residents brooded?
19. Mil. address
20. Domicile: abbr.
21. 1962 hit subtitled "That Kiss!"
22. Old-fashioned business letter salutation
24. Beauty pageant toppers
26. "One Flew Over the Cuckoo's Nest" author
28. British WWII-era gun
29. Flounder's cousin
33. ___ Angeles
35. "___ while we're on the subject. . . "
36. He killed Abel
37. Generous Holland folks provided dinner?
42. Prefix with space or dynamic
43. "Gotcha!"
44. ___ or nothing
45. Metric weight
46. Moolah
48. Bloodsucker
52. "___ Place," 1957 Lana Turner movie
54. Have the nerve
55. Amber-colored beer
59. Pro bono ad: abbr.
61. Census category
62. Parisians sizzled last summer?
65. Aide: abbr.
66. Govt. home financing org.
67. Folk singer Guthrie
68. Topers
69. Part of an udder
70. Low voice

Down

1. Common TV dinner
2. Absolutely despises
3. Gaming cube
4. Mix, as cake batter
5. Crucial situation
6. Santa's syllables
7. Intrinsic
8. Prophetess of Greek myth
9. Commoner: abbr.
10. Sewing machine inventor Elias
11. Scores 100 percent
12. Kind of list
17. Eligible for a pension, maybe abbr.
18. How-___ (helpful books)
19. Inquire
23. Rarely
25. Stopped
27. "I love ___"
29. Climbed, as a mountain
30. Feedbag morsel
31. Prevaricate
32. Termination
34. Play director's exit destination
37. "You're it!" chasing game
38. That girl
39. Pitcher's stat
40. Native American Montana people
41. Pipe joint
47. Formal headgear
49. Painters' stands
50. Principle statements
51. Evil spell
52. ___ for the course
53. Letters on a bounced check
55. School orgs.
56. "I see," facetiously
57. "___ we forget"
58. Small salamanders
60. Swift, compact horse
63. Nashville-based awards org.
64. Bank nest egg, initially

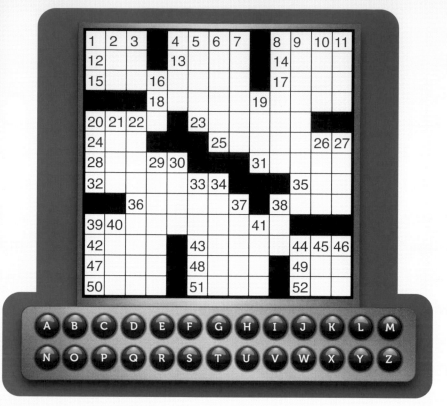

Comic Hero to Movie Star

Across

1. "Pimp My Ride" network
4. Whole note's lack
8. PC key
12. Split ___ soup
13. County seat of Allen County, Kansas
14. Mandolin kin
15. Classical language of India
17. Karenina of literature
18. Comic book hero played by Nicolas Cage
20. Bunch of feathers
23. Jungle queen of comics
24. ___ -Locka, Florida
25. Made changes to
28. Comic book hero played by Sylvester Stallone, with 31-Across
31. See 28-Across
32. Make go
35. PBS funder
36. Blunt
38. Loads of
39. Comic book hero played by Dick Durock
42. Minnesota neighbor
43. Circles
47. Gillette's ___ II razor
48. "Catch!"
49. Biol. evidence
50. Scottish island
51. Belgian river
52. Quaint

Down

1. Army arresters: abbr.
2. Brewed beverage
3. Airport-shuttle vehicle
4. Follower of Guru Nanak
5. Bullfight competitors
6. Bible prophet
7. Barbie's company
8. Less ornate
9. Former home of the Cleveland Cavaliers

10. "___ Reader" (eclectic magazine)
11. Bartlett or Anjou
16. Warrant officer's inferior: abbr.
19. No longer in service: abbr.
20. Japanese WWII general
21. Start of a Fifth Dimension tune or a Superman departure
22. Gradually disappeared
26. The first garden
27. WWII turning point
29. Possible reaction to bad news
30. Tombstone lawman Wyatt
33. Easily annoyed
34. Reverberates
37. Solution strength, in Surrey

38. Joe Torre, e.g.: abbr.
39. Joins a jury
40. Function
41. Poetic negative
44. A bachelor's last words?
45. Conclude
46. Bummed out

Things Are Heating Up

Across

1. Pottery class gunk
4. Drain the energy from
7. Actresses Evans and Hamilton
13. Opp. of WSW
14. President's time in office
16. Tiny critter seen on a slide
17. U.S. spy org.
18. Nobel winner Harold who discovered heavy hydrogen
19. Suggested indirectly
20. Little consolation
23. Summer in Paris
24. Clownish action
25. Western Hemisphere org.
26. Mo. after Mar.
28. One who stays calm during a tense situation
33. Game with Professor Plum
36. "___ to Joy"
37. Common way to fortify table salt
38. Fled
39. Chant sounds
40. Hockey great Bobby
41. Org. that sticks to its guns
42. Pay what is owed
44. Bullring cheer
45. Walrus relative
46. Not be a first-string player
49. "___ about time!"
50. ___ glance
51. Partner of aahed
55. Unit of electrical resistance
57. Passionate
60. Realm
62. Prefix for logy or gram
63. First U.S. st.
64. ___ million
65. CNN offering
66. Period
67. Turn the color of a beet
68. Queue after Q
69. Happy for glad: abbr.

Down

1. Holy city of Islam
2. Teamsters, e.g.
3. Did a poker task
4. Wall plaster
5. Early plane prefix
6. Casts a shape in advance
7. Cowardly Lion portrayer Bert
8. One who mimics
9. "Smoking or ___?"
10. Decide conclusively
11. Help in a crime
12. Marquis de ___
15. "Get outta ___!" ("Stop hassling me!")
21. Craps cubes

22. Big Ten sch.
27. Pea holder
29. Energy or enthusiasm
30. Ambulance wail
31. Poet Pound
32. Actual
33. Gullet
34. Actress Turner
35. Like some beards or Christmas trees
39. Do better than
40. Shrub also known as a rose bay
43. Paramedic: abbr.
44. Get
45. Loafer, e.g.
47. Dine

48. Kelly to Regis
52. Lord of the underworld
53. Each
54. Raspy singer Bob
55. Smell
56. Sharpen, as a knife
58. Put ___ act (pretend)
59. Mountain drinks?
61. Help

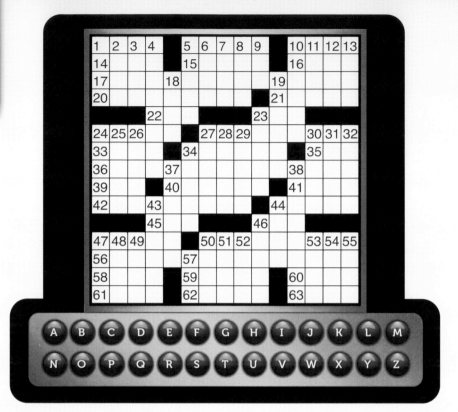

The International Scene

Across

1. Ooze
5. Excuse
10. Soothing ointment
14. Summon
15. A difficulty or complication
16. Double-reed woodwind
17. They're fiercer than city apes
20. Member speaking for the whole ball team
21. Lacks
22. Not straight
23. Untidy place
24. Performer
27. This gun for hire
33. Central part
34. Military barracks
35. Quilting party, perhaps
36. Countries just hatched
39. Turn over the engine
40. National song
41. Quote or mention
42. White-collar bag
44. Cuts from copy
45. "___ Were King"
46. Defeater of the Luftwaffe: abbr.
47. Nappy leather
50. Mermaids have them
56. Controlled by the military
58. German river or dam
59. God's fishbowl
60. Peru's capital
61. Boys
62. Squeeze in
63. Observed

Down

1. Atlantic porgy
2. Supreme Court Justice Warren
3. Noted island prison
4. Theater lover
5. Quite incensed
6. Turn down: var.
7. Fixe or reçue: Fr.

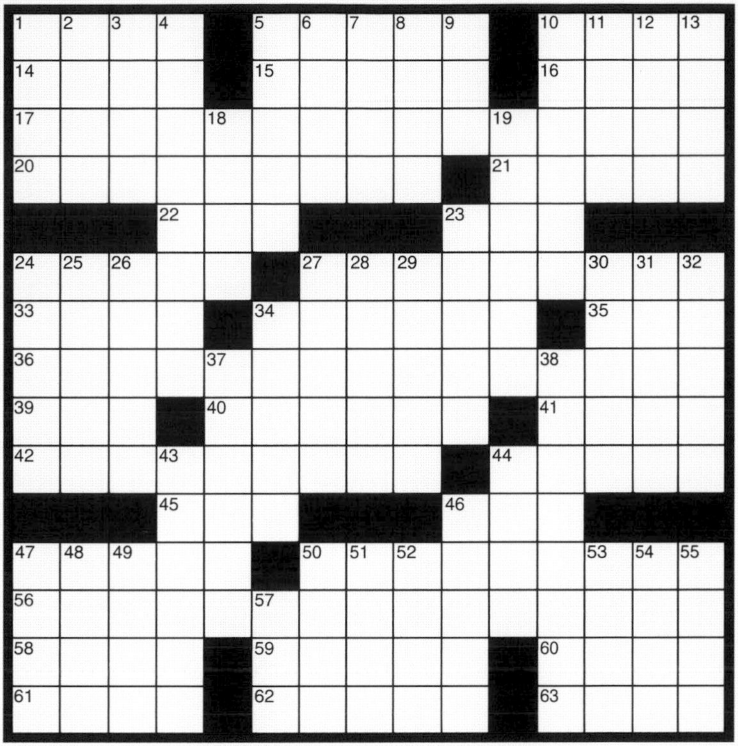

8. Expel air
9. Middle East country: abbr.
10. Henry's Anne
11. Fit
12. Burden
13. Army meal
18. Close
19. Meaning
23. Beat it!
24. Sharp and biting
25. Person on way to success
26. Famous fountain of Rome
27. Devilfish
28. Baltic natives
29. Opera's Fleming
30. Seething
31. French income
32. Affirmatives
34. Beatrice, "The Beautiful Parricide"
37. Lighting director
38. Chunks dropping off glaciers
43. Downy ducks
44. Computer input or output
46. Class of German wines
47. Takes to court
48. Loosen a knot
49. Happy place
50. Confront
51. Steamed
52. Men only
53. Mr. Nastase
54. Feeble, as an excuse
55. Singer of one last song
57. Shorten the grass

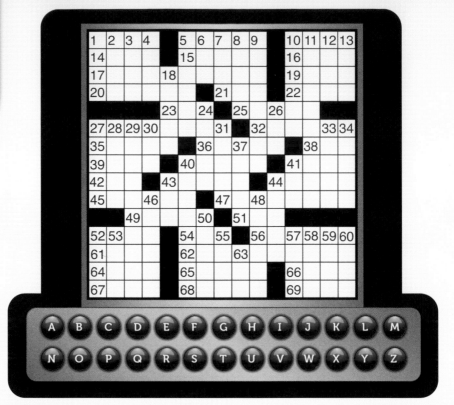

Gram's Birthday

Across

1. Dangerous when it flows
5. He wrote "The Stars and Stripes Forever"
10. Like a senior citizen
14. Milton wrote them
15. Surrounding atmospheres
16. Sideless cart
17. Small units of weight
19. Unusual
20. Chant
21. Law: Fr.
22. Mean little kids
23. Branch of the service: abbr.
25. Northeastern state of India
27. Enroll
32. Comb. of high cards
35. The Southwest's Bret
36. Actress Debra
38. Reagan, to friends
39. Ages
40. Sprayed defensively
41. If it's "half," it's small
42. Where to get $$: abbr.
43. Welfare allotments
44. Civil War general
45. Oklahoman
47. Kitchen utensil
49. Showers with stones
51. Eternally: poet.
52. Sounds of laughter
54. Once ___ blue moon
56. Things to eat
61. Smell
62. Heart examination
64. Eat
65. Silkworms
66. Tear down: sp. var.
67. English monetary abbreviation
68. Coarse grass
69. Tennis stadium honoree

Down

1. Places
2. Between Yemen and Oman
3. Escape port for air

The crossword grid with numbered cells: 1, 2, 3, 4, 5, 6, 7, 8, 9, 10, 11, 12, 13, 14, 15, 16, 17, 18, 19, 20, 21, 22, 23, 24, 25, 26, 27, 28, 29, 30, 31, 32, 33, 34, 35, 36, 37, 38, 39, 40, 41, 42, 43, 44, 45, 46, 47, 48, 49, 50, 51, 52, 53, 54, 55, 56, 57, 58, 59, 60, 61, 62, 63, 64, 65, 66, 67, 68, 69.

4. Regarding
5. Wisest
6. Belonging to us
7. ___ Mountains
8. Where R.L.S. died
9. Helped
10. Name of six popes
11. Parser
12. Wyatt ___
13. Colors
18. Sign on a lab door
24. Himalayan kingdom
26. Part of a tennis match
27. Flightless birds
28. "An ___ the ground"
29. Record player

30. Possessive pronoun
31. "The Camptown ___"
33. Spanish earl
34. "Abandon hope, all ye who ___ here" (Dante)
37. "Beau ___"
40. Tenons' companions
41. Charlottetown is its capital: abbr.
43. Singer Shannon
44. Driver Andretti
46. Closer
48. Edit
50. Trap
52. Devices for carrying bricks
53. Mine entrance

55. Sere
57. Taj Mahal city
58. Depression agencies: abbr.
59. One of "The Incredibles"
60. Duck
63. Hammarskjöld

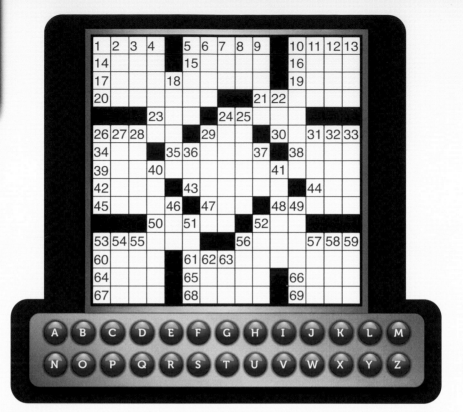

Animal House

Across

1. Concordes: abbr.
5. Bass and treble
10. Teases
14. Lotion additive
15. Aged: Lat.
16. Concerning: Lat.
17. Biggest portion
19. Amateur sports group: abbr.
20. Editor's equipment
21. Owl hours
23. Paul, the guitar guy
24. Ready supply
26. Greek physician
29. Exclude
30. ___ plea (pleads guilty): sl.
34. Military address: abbr.
35. Greek flier
38. Pinches
39. Ivy League team
42. Ireland
43. Fuel vessel
44. Regret
45. Lots and lots: var.
47. Kleindienst, Kennedy, Civiletti, etc.: abbr.
48. Beginning
50. O'Casey and Connery
52. One: Fr.
53. Dan, former CBS newsman
56. Mournful
60. Surrounding atmosphere
61. String game
64. Put away
65. Wipe out
66. Young adult
67. Make like a goose
68. Put off
69. Orient

Down

1. Mineo and Maglie
2. Sales receipt
3. Implement
4. Mentally deteriorated
5. Examples
6. Annealing oven

7. Timetable heading: abbr.
8. Distant
9. Office skill, for short
10. Giant simian
11. Traverse little by little
12. Mild oath
13. Oceans
18. Like some views
22. Transport watchdogs: abbr.
24. East Indian dresses
25. Ring apparel
26. Stares open mouthed
27. March follower
28. French river
29. WWII battle site
31. Breakwaters

32. Mold opening
33. Plus quality
36. That: Fr.
37. Sault ___ Marie
40. Reporter
41. Presser
46. Match the bet
49. Nullify
51. Curved
52. Worrier's worry
53. Allergic evidence
54. Manual's companion, for short
55. 1982 animated Disney feature
56. Being: Lat.
57. Concept

58. Pub drinks
59. Penny
62. 100 square meters
63. Make lace

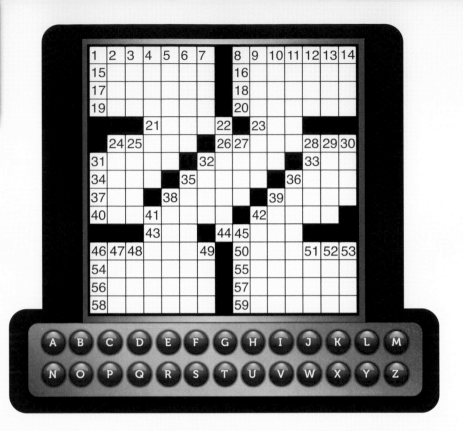

Sevens

Across

1. Gowns
8. Sedative
15. Distributed the deck again
16. Akin
17. Ready, willing, ___
18. Standing up
19. More tired
20. Speeder's speed, perhaps
21. Queen ___ lace
23. Melody
24. Walks nervously
26. Guiding light
31. Mists
32. Antisocial one
33. One ___ time
34. Six make an inning
35. Lawn machine
36. Story basis
37. Exploit
38. Paddy crops
39. Monotonous hum
40. Give a second examination
42. Actress Dunne
43. Cinder
44. Sagas
46. Brainier
50. Kitchen appliance
54. Italian dessert
55. Citrus drink
56. Changed
57. Warned
58. Yellowstone attractions
59. Deteriorates

Down

1. Sketch
2. Philosopher Descartes
3. Norse epic
4. Some regattas
5. Roman victims of 290 B.C.
6. Burstyn and DeGeneres
7. Cubic meter
8. Bikini halves
9. He enjoys novels twice
10. Famed portrayer of Hamlet
11. Microwave devices

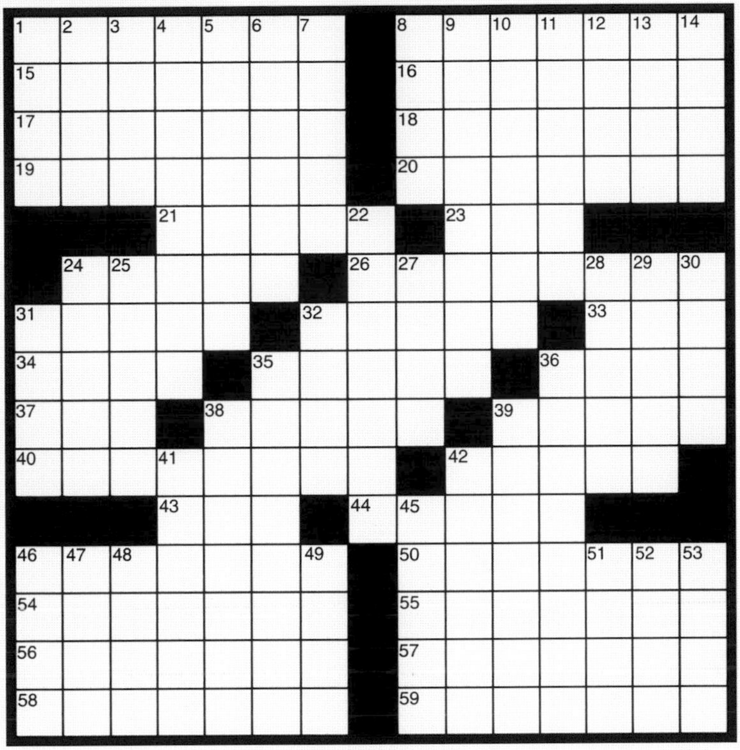

12. To put ___ a nutshell…
13. Impression
14. Nervous
22. Most snaillike
24. Take a short break
25. Mexican native
27. Wallet fillers
28. Claw
29. Make amends
30. Velocity
31. Time unit
32. Door feature
35. Author of "The Covenant"
36. Mangle operators
38. Make like new
39. Visionary
41. Author Bret, et al.
42. Philippines city
45. Counselor-___
46. Buck
47. Burrower
48. Bohemian
49. Frees (of)
51. London gallery
52. Actress Barbara
53. Ohio team

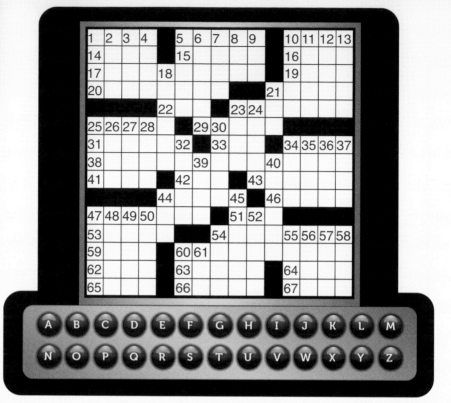

Picket Line

Across

1. Creole veggie
5. Spread seed
10. Strategy
14. Hyena's hideaway
15. $100 bill
16. Lounge (around)
17. Arrest at an English school?
19. Wistful word
20. Avoid
21. Type of drum
22. Fed. retirement agency
23. Grumbles
25. Snake charmer's pet
29. Book after Micah
31. Like a short play
33. Stephen of "V for Vendetta"
34. Sailor's greeting
38. Sarandon and Sontag after a fight?
41. Collection of computer bits
42. Legal matter
43. Before the deadline
44. "Then again, I could be wrong"
46. Track athlete
47. Tex-Mex eats
51. Splashy resort
53. Eyeball-bending paintings
54. Guess-the-murderer story
59. Lawn additive
60. Picket line at Shea Stadium?
62. ___ instant
63. When repeated, a word of solace
64. Annoys
65. Lascivious look
66. Dad's sisters
67. Makes known

Down

1. Designer Cassini
2. Winslet of "Finding Neverland"
3. Run amok
4. Pisa's river
5. Macbeth and Duncan, e.g.

6. To be returned
7. Kind of whistle
8. JFK posting
9. Austrian article
10. Drawing-board original
11. Bochco legal drama
12. Arkansas's ___ Mountains
13. Flunkies' responses
18. John of "Being John Malkovich"
21. Addition solution
23. Tool building
24. Kind of
25. Ty or Lee J.
26. Nothing but
27. Ready to hit the hay

28. Marathon, for one
30. Playground retort
32. ___ cotta
34. Home of some bubbly
35. Precipitation pellets
36. Treater's words
37. River to the North Sea
39. Wants
40. Like a messy bed
44. Famed ballplayer Mel
45. Souvenir shop item
47. Manuscript leaf
48. Mimic's forte
49. Actor Malcolm- ___ Warner
50. Ryan of "The Beverly Hillbillies"

52. Proverbial pig containers
54. Architect with an avian name
55. Banned submachine guns
56. Nick's partner
57. Like a Parker?
58. Lass in a Hardy tale
60. RR terminal
61. Wed. follower

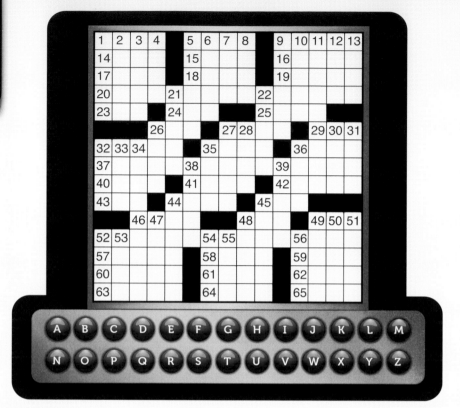

Famous Fare

Across

1. Tortoiselike
5. Word with wrench or dream
9. Medieval weapons
14. Ice shape
15. Yemeni port
16. Actress Verdugo
17. Top draft status
18. Furnish temporarily
19. Wise legislator
20. Loved dairy product?
23. Hosp. areas
24. Voice-man Blanc
25. Pianist Dame Myra
26. Lush surroundings?
27. Nairobi Trio players
29. Howard Hughes's airline
32. Frequently
35. Spread unit
36. Famous twins' birthplace
37. Comedic pastry?
40. Summer coolers
41. Attention-getter
42. Argument flaws
43. Kind of party
44. Tucked in for the night
45. Director's cry
46. The Police was one
48. Norm's bartender
49. Convened
52. Soul food dessert?
57. Pertaining to surface extent
58. Ajar
59. Hennery
60. Recipe instruction
61. One side of a 1973 ruling
62. Whet
63. Roman social sites
64. Luge, e.g.
65. Lyric poems

Down

1. Twenty
2. Type of month
3. Heeds
4. Don
5. Four-time Masters champ

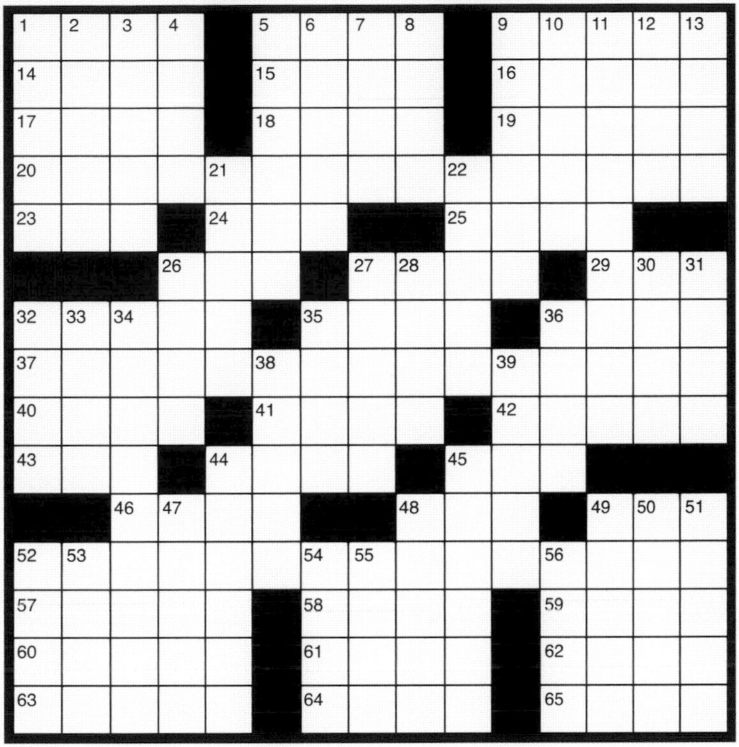

(Crossword grid)

6. Perfect example
7. Historic Quaker
8. Prefix meaning "inside"
9. Interlocks
10. Fleshy medicinal plants
11. Heavenly
12. Cain's nephew
13. Rational
21. Certain sultanate citizen
22. Root in the stands
26. They must be covered
    to be real
27. Hurt plenty
28. Spring event
30. Aftermath

31. "My Cup Runneth Over"
    singer Ed
32. Leave out
33. Confront
34. Doctor's specialty
35. Former Davis Cup captain
36. Glaswegian, e.g.
38. Big shot
39. Tack type
44. Ushers' milieus
45. Sacked
47. Extend
48. Nobel, e.g.
49. Rose
50. Offer reparation
51. Genres

52. Entrance part
53. Diva's piece
54. Spats
55. Fall birthstone
56. Reverberate

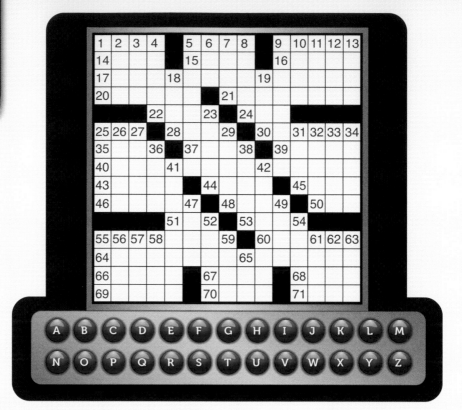

Let's Face the Music

Across

1. Herr von Bismarck
5. Skin doctor's field: abbr.
9. Aptly named fruit
14. "If I may be so bold..."
15. Neighborhood
16. Girl rescued by Don Juan
17. He wrote what was originally called "Defense of Fort M'Henry" in 1814
20. 1968 hit with the lyric "I like the way you walk, I like the way you talk"
21. Prepares text for publication
22. Split pea, e.g.
24. Private address?
25. Econ. yardstick
28. Feed holder
30. Large sea ducks
35. 1964 Oscar-winning actress Kedrova
37. Deep grooves
39. Earth's path
40. "More optimistically..."
43. Sheer curtain fabric
44. Red Cross supplies
45. Slow flow
46. Make beloved
48. Seldom seen
50. "The Spanish Tragedy" dramatist
51. Pro's opposite
53. International org. since 1881
55. Floral ornaments
60. Down Under denizen
64. Seismology tool
66. Kid's song refrain
67. Place in order
68. RAM unit
69. Philosopher Kierkegaard
70. WWW addresses
71. Miss Trueheart, of old comics

Down

1. Clumsy sorts

92

2. Drive-___ window
3. Afternoon socials
4. Bygone Dodge models
5. Iced rum cocktail
6. Hospital trauma centers: abbr.
7. Nap, maybe
8. "Miracle on 34th Street" store
9. Like some motives
10. Obtains
11. Cotton to
12. "Okay if ___ myself out?"
13. What Simon does, in a
   kids' game
18. Industry big shots: abbr.
19. Early Ron Howard role
23. Outlet inserts

25. Hand protector
26. Smooth, sheer fabric
27. Kilt's pattern, often
29. Miscellaneous category
31. First 007 movie
32. Online library offering
33. Snazzy
34. Spirited mount
36. Competent
38. Wander off the path
41. Stimulus response
42. Sets aside (for)
47. Campus military org.
49. Old 5-franc pieces
52. Associate of Gandhi
54. Fancy tie

55. AAA travel recommendations
56. The Buckeye State
57. Crystal ball studier
58. New York canal
59. Headliner
61. Rational
62. Spots in the Seine
63. Mouse-sighting shrieks
65. Photo blow-up: abbr.

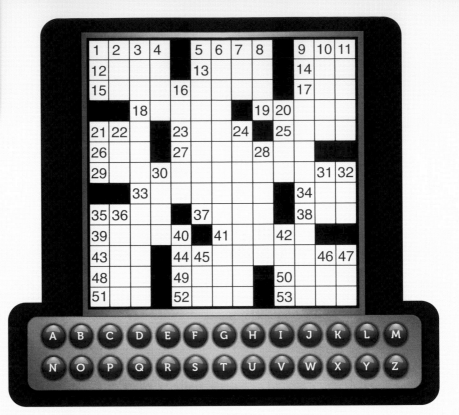

A Little Bit of Everything

Across

1. Bar tallies
5. Included in an e-mail
9. Middle of a game
12. The rain in Spain
13. River connected to the Tiber by a canal
14. Org. with TKOs
15. Relative of Old Man Winter?
17. "Son of," to a Saudi
18. Something to play for
19. Beast of Borden
21. Pool stick
23. Part of a 3-piece suit
25. News for a gossip columnist
26. Poop deck's place
27. Chef's creations
29. "Lions for Lambs" director
33. Closes back up
34. Dijon dissent
35. Go under
37. Get under the skin of
38. Seventh out of 24, Greek-style
39. Midlife crisis symptom
41. Brother on "Frasier"
43. ___ voce (with one voice)
44. Reels from a punch
48. Homer's neighbor
49. Land measure
50. Cream, for one
51. Bunyan's tool
52. "Star Trek" actor Tim
53. Singer-songwriter Tori

Down

1. Muslim's cap
2. Muslim general, especially in Turkey
3. Old firefighting method
4. Samurai's quaff
5. Many a builder
6. Athletic shoes
7. Lowest commissioned rank in U.S. Navy: abbr.
8. Shower with fondness
9. Is coercive

94

10. Angie's role on "Law & Order"
11. "Cave ___!" ("Beware of the dog!")
16. High temperatures
20. Willingly
21. Word after used or touring
22. Visiting alien vessel
24. Climbers for creepers
28. Old Fords
30. Swimmers with toxic blood
31. Deteriorate
32. Chain material
35. Animal wildlife
36. Take over, as territory
40. Nicholas II was the last one

42. "Tell Mama" singer James
45. Old French coin
46. A "Road" picture destination for Bob and Bing
47. Urgent cry for help

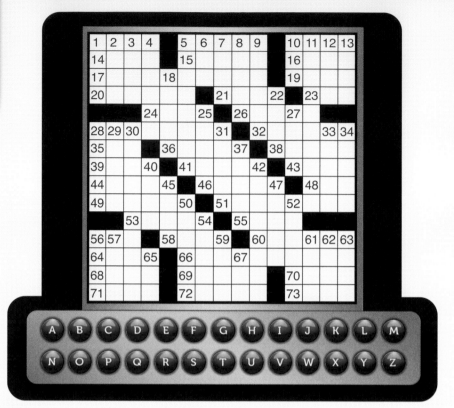

All Mixed Up

Across

1. Kind of list
5. Pasta topper
10. Fence the goods, say
14. Moonfish
15. Forearm bones
16. Lose brightness
17. Aviator pleads?
19. Forest unit
20. Said it wasn't so
21. Salty septet
23. Terminus
24. Orch. section
26. Bombing on stage
28. "Slammin'" golf legend
32. Prepares clams, perhaps
35. Turkish honorific
36. Music-maker's org.
38. Whom Bugs bugs
39. Hound sound
41. Bush
43. Light tune
44. Offer one's two cents
46. "Like a Rock" rocker
48. Museum-funding org.
49. Domingo and others
51. Alcoves
53. Leaves
55. Meter maid leavings: abbr.
56. Massages elicit them
58. A pop
60. Many John Wayne movies
64. Anger, and then some
66. 17-Across, 11-Down, and 30-Down—all mixed up
68. [Sigh]
69. Thrusting weapon
70. Speak with vitriol
71. Flappers' hairdos
72. Urged, with "on"
73. Certain NCOs

Down

1. Swamp critter
2. Mayberry kid
3. "Aw, heck!"

4. "Excuse me, waitress?"
5. Summer outfit
6. Priest's robe
7. French articles
8. Like some parrots
9. University application parts
10. Toward the stern
11. Naked urchins?
12. First place?
13. Prepared for driving
18. Insurance giant
22. Location
25. Goldman's partner on Wall Street
27. "Little" Dickens girl
28. Wooden shoe

29. Wide open
30. Leathernecks chat?
31. Risk-taker
33. Free-for-all
34. Puerto Rican misses: abbr.
37. Washington's ___ Sound
40. Fort with a fortune
42. Summoned
45. Buffalo's lake
47. Change the price, maybe
50. Horse home
52. Cool red giants in the sky
54. Scrawny one
56. Swift, compact horse
57. Heavenly overhead?
59. Suspend

61. Online periodical
62. Monthly payment for some
63. Retired jets: abbr.
65. Slalom curve
67. Cooler contents

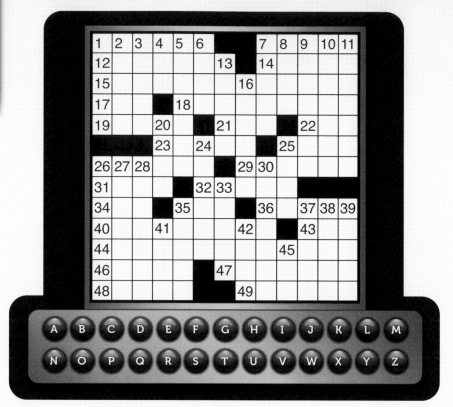

Studio 54

Across

1. Spin
7. Partner of pains
12. Complete miss
14. Rake over the coals
15. Makeup of edible Scottie dogs
17. Breakfast partner
18. Act like an icicle?
19. That is, Latin
21. ___ Saint-Louis
22. Onetime BMT rival
23. 2001 International Tennis Hall of Fame inductee
25. Presidential act
26. Sacred place
29. Opposed
31. Denial from Putin
32. Fruit implement
34. Truly, madly, or deeply: abbr.
35. Open-house org.
36. Assaulted
40. Readied, as a range
43. Bear a grudge against
44. Cash holder
46. Slanting
47. Not as firm
48. Manages
49. Exceedingly bad

Down

1. Teacher of a sort
2. Snockered
3. Kind of union
4. "Ugly Betty" network
5. "Break time!"
6. Poet ___ Wheeler Wilcox
7. Left one's bunk
8. Wood measure
9. More frightening
10. Guides
11. Sanford's British inspiration
13. Furious
16. Subterranean chamber
20. Skirt feature
24. Sugar-rich liquid
25. Norm's wife on "Cheers"
26. Rebukes sharply

1	2	3	4	5	6			7	8	9	10	11
12						13		14				
15							16					
17				18								
19			20			21			22			
		23		24				25				
26	27	28					29	30				
31				32	33							
34			35				36		37	38	39	
40		41				42		43				
44							45					
46					47							
48					49							

27. Add moisture to
28. Really relish
30. Guilty, e.g.
33. Many a Hoot Gibson picture
35. Vexatious people
37. Out
38. End of a Beatles song title
39. Monty Python member Gilliam
41. Word following privately or hand
42. Garry Trudeau's "Check Your ___ at the Door"
45. Runner, of sorts

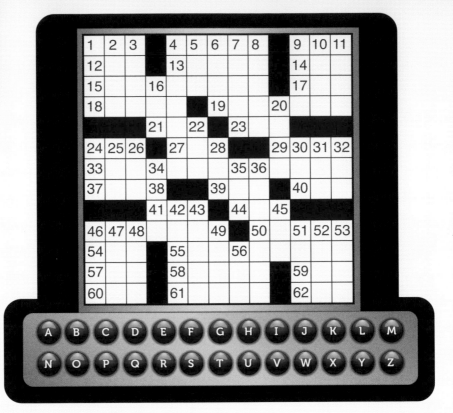

Not in the Dairy Case

Across

1. Testing site
4. Absorb, as gravy
9. Cadge
12. ___ Miss
13. Command to a lifter
14. Seek office
15. Variety of squash
17. "This American Life" host Glass
18. Net receipts?
19. Major shipbuilding city
21. "The Happy ___" (Harry Connick, Jr., holiday song)
23. It may be blonde
24. Cable TV network
27. ". . . and seven years ___ . . ."
29. Emblem on Canada's flag
33. Candy bar ingredient
37. Bridge
39. "The lowest form of humour": Samuel Johnson
40. Color in Canada's flag
41. Tree used for chair seats
44. Women's article of clothing
46. Temporary window replacement, sometimes
50. Off the cuff
54. Kia subcompact
55. Fountain offering
57. Bollix
58. Take control of
59. AC/DC lead singer ___ Scott
60. Run off at the mouth
61. Classic battle participants
62. Long in the tooth

Down

1. Brain region
2. Reunion attendee, briefly
3. Kind of software release
4. Natural plastic
5. Done, to Donne
6. Hunger pain
7. Tongue neighbor

8. Colorful part of a plant
9. Guardhouse
10. Currency adopted by Slovenia in 2007
11. Chew like a beaver
16. Cause of sudden death?
20. Put on the market
22. E-tail?
24. Lecture no-nos
25. Thimbleful
26. Newbery Medal org.
28. Alley ending?
30. Listening device
31. Had some food
32. Gave some food to
34. Felt sure about

35. Baby lion
36. Freeway access points
42. Center of power
43. Code which bears inventor's name
45. Promotions
46. Michael Crichton novel
47. Former currency of Turkey
48. Prince Andrew's dukedom
49. Caen couple
51. University of New Mexico athlete
52. Graven image
53. Rubber or brass follower
56. "Two heads ___ better than one"

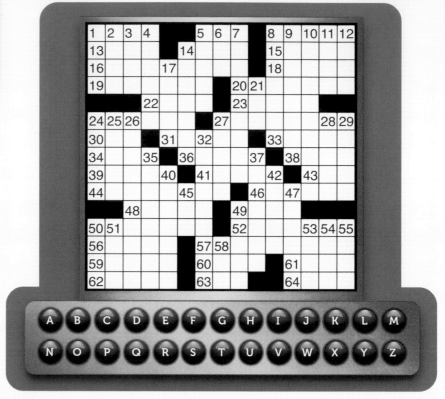

As You Will

Across

1. Summer getaway
5. Choke off a cry
8. Sail supports
13. Khayyám
14. Elephant boy of the movies
15. Former USSR cooperative
16. It might be for better or worse
18. Meadow overpass
19. Rivals at war
20. Marked
22. Levin and Gershwin
23. "I get ___ out of you . . ."
24. Appear to do well
27. Estop, in law
30. Boston watch-word: abbr.
31. Actress Eleonora, et al.
33. Photo tone
34. Diamond or Young
36. Jumping sticks
38. Atmospheric pollution
39. Dais principal
41. Mountains of Utah
43. Summer quaff
44. Wrestling maneuver
46. Thinker, in a way
48. "The bald ___" (Dogpatch denizen)
49. Opposed, in 48-Across locale
50. Tests for better results
52. Milksops
56. Foreclose on ___
57. Be encouraged
59. Cohered
60. Flock members
61. Line a roof
62. Etta's cartoon relatives
63. Type of alert
64. A dish for José

Down

1. Where coos are heard
2. "___ for All Seasons"
3. Manufacture
4. Early newborn, for short
5. Electromagnetic unit

6. Cut short: abbr.
7. Icelandic poet who wrote in Danish
8. Gummy substances
9. Items
10. Mugger, of a kind
11. Scope or photo start
12. Kane's Rosebud
14. Become misty
17. Ventilated
21. Greek or Turkish weight
24. Pulitzer poet: 1929
25. Swelling
26. Stand pat
27. Schoolyard game, ___ the ring
28. Vacuum tube
29. Excited
32. Tar's gear
35. Opposing generals or actress's full name
37. Smokes
40. Ruchings, e.g.
42. Foolishly imitative
45. Grand ___ Opry
47. Katydid, for one
49. Questioned
50. Pool hall equipment
51. She: Fr.
53. UN-related group centered in Vienna: abbr.
54. Novelist Ambler
55. Town on the Vire
58. Overwhelm

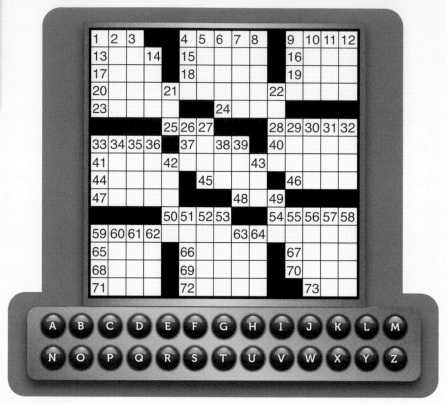

In Other Words

Across

1. Literary collection
4. Ruin's partner
9. Rebuke
13. Decrease
15. Consumed
16. A little, in music
17. Greedy
18. Got up
19. Type of chamber
20. Notarial cheater, in other words
23. Overjoy
24. Final
25. Free
28. Listens to
33. Sweep's foe
37. Ruler on the Rialto
40. Actor Davis
41. Mutilate scepter, in other words
44. Marie Antoinette, e.g.
45. Jannings or Ludwig
46. Tibetan oxen
47. Plus
48. Pinch
50. Koufax stats: abbr.
54. Odor
59. Braille primrose, in other words
65. Country on the Caspian
66. Like some skirts
67. Dross
68. Average
69. Growing out
70. Bingo kin
71. Mound builders
72. Stymie
73. NYSE purchase: abbr.

Down

1. Cognizant
2. Of the seagoing service
3. Loos or O'Day
4. End of dependence
5. ___ avis: Lat.
6. Semicircular island

7. Jai alai equipment
8. On hands and ___
9. Risky investment: abbr.
10. Arm of a firth
11. Feel every muscle
12. Down and out
14. Emend
21. Above: poet.
22. One of three swordsmen
26. Mt. ___, Crete
27. Love lavishly
29. Spot
30. On the main
31. Casablanca nightclub owner
32. Complete outfits
33. Koran section

34. Cheers for Ferdinand
35. "Miss ___ Regrets"
36. Prong
38. Precious stone
39. Land of loughs
42. Foot, for Frost
43. Actor Wallach
49. Anderson or Tillis
51. Stormed
52. Favorite Garbo word
53. Jack of rhyme
55. Take a chance
56. Famous Canadian physician
57. Signified
58. Peloponnesian city
59. Mona ___

60. ___ horse
61. Phloem
62. Grandson of the first family
63. Network
64. Baltic feeder

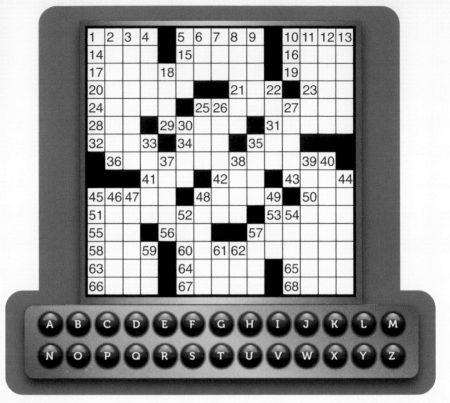

The Hard Stuff

Across

1. Mosquito or fly
5. Hula skirt material
10. Swelled heads
14. Something to think about
15. Crimean seaport
16. Have too little
17. Venomous snake
19. Fashion magazine
20. Combining form meaning "in front"
21. By means of
23. Alley- ___ (basketball play)
24. Grinch creator
25. Sharp mind, figuratively
28. Imbibe daintily
29. Inventor Howe
31. Actress Ryan
32. Stewpot: Sp.
34. Belief system
35. Tall president, for short
36. It's a sure thing
41. Dorm VIPs
42. Summer hours in N.Y.C.
43. Site for a bell
45. For this purpose only: Lat.
48. Chord type
50. Li'l Abner's Daisy ___
51. Old name for a locomotive
53. Arab leaders
55. Neighbor of Israel: abbr.
56. Suffix with diction
57. Response to a naysayer
58. "Schindler's List" star Neeson
60. Billionaire's girlfriend, maybe
63. Behold to Brutus
64. Licorice-flavored plant
65. Give the old heave-ho to
66. Gone out with
67. Hornets' homes
68. Decides on, with "for"

Down

1. Painter Pablo
2. Al Bundy on "Married . . . with Children"

3. Consisting of seven parts
4. Saves for later viewing
5. Greek sandwich
6. Stadium noise
7. Pub offering
8. Forestalls, with "off"
9. Dogpatch denizen Hawkins
10. Meadow mama
11. Aplenty
12. To be returned
13. Treeless tract
18. Celtic language
22. Suspect's story
25. Spanish ayes
26. Interferes, as with evidence
27. General drift

30. "My ___ are sealed"
33. Composer Copland
35. Court records
37. Cottage for Putin
38. Actress Falco
39. Arising
40. Most raspy
44. Vacation spots
45. Nuptial paths
46. Frozen carbon dioxide
47. Mann of education
48. "Taste this"
49. Metric prefix
52. Kind of transplant
54. Myopic cartoon character
57. Fateful day

59. Word on a door
61. Fleur-de- ___
62. "Spring ahead" syst.

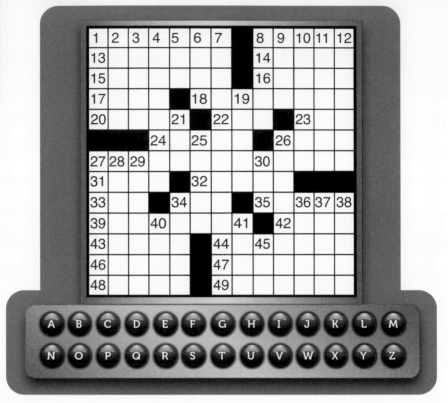

Mail Service

Across

1. Achieve through deception
8. Native Israeli
13. "Told you so"
14. Really dug
15. Chump
16. Smiling
17. ___ Conner, Miss USA 2006
18. Seemed likely
20. Tonto's horse
22. Wade opponent
23. Emergency med. procedure
24. Sings the praises of
26. Obligation
27. Business address, perhaps
31. Parliamentary procedures?
32. Hubbub
33. KITT or General Lee
34. New Deal monogram
35. Emulated a sous chef
39. Tree carvings
42. Malcolm Arnold's "Fantasy for Cello," for example
43. Fabrications
44. Best possible
46. Latin clarifier
47. Childlike attitude
48. Gives off, as light
49. Met at the door

Down

1. Partner of figures
2. Violinist Stern
3. Part of TNT
4. Attacks
5. Disparity
6. Tale-teller
7. "American History X" star
8. Noncom's nickname
9. Plugging away
10. Den denizen
11. Approach quickly
12. Bird in "B.C."
19. Polite refusal
21. Chinese ideal
25. Norwegian "ouch"

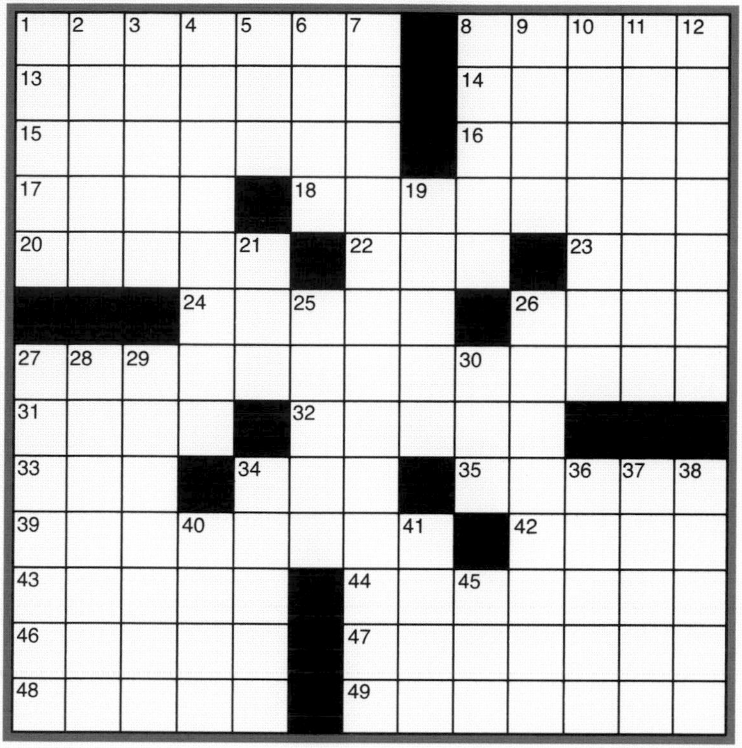

26. Putting down
27. Promoting peace
28. National anthem since 1980
29. Three make a turkey
30. Potential bait-taker
34. Bruce Lee's weapons
36. Doomsday cause, perhaps
37. Fill with happiness
38. Handed (out)
40. Experiment
41. Category of crystals
45. Casual Friday omission

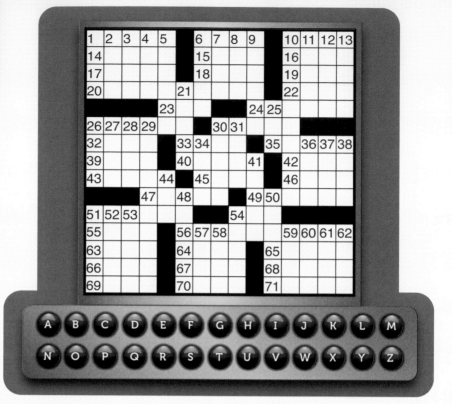

Mister Ed-ucation

Across

1. Admit
6. Reverse or neutral
10. Norwegian metropolis
14. From Rome: pref.
15. Crucifix inscription
16. Atop of
17. Take it off
18. Rivers of comedy
19. Price displayers
20. Cuties that lack depth?
22. Garfield's sidekick
23. Raw metal
24. Trick shot in a film, e.g.
26. Visit briefly
30. Emphatic turndown
32. Duct drop
33. Sky sightings
35. Horizontal line on a graph
39. K-12, textbook-wise
40. Kind of tournament
42. Storied captain
43. Cap attachment
45. New Age music superstar
46. Nibble, beaver style
47. Weather, in a way
49. Wishful thinking
51. Boardroom echoes
54. "Diamonds ___ Forever"
55. Keen on
56. Mister Ed-ucation?
63. Alt.
64. Part of a Faulkner title
65. Online letters
66. Superman's lady
67. Model airplane builder's need
68. Capone colleague
69. Fashion's Christian
70. Sentry's cry
71. Elders and alders

Down

1. Talk like Daffy Duck
2. Place in a Robert Redford movie
3. Canvas covering
4. Former netman Nastase

5. "Piece of cake"
6. Toy soldier
7. Chemical compound
8. Uzbekistan border sea
9. Salon jobs
10. Where to take the roast?
11. Bogart sleuth
12. Mr. Spock's strong suit
13. Advent
21. Wither
25. Tricky situation
26. Remarriage prefix
27. Fabled archer
28. Surfer's paradise
29. Top van driver?
30. Everybody's opposite
31. Anthem opening
34. Ricky's landlord
36. "___: Warrior Princess"
37. Mosque V.I.P.
38. Pen mothers
41. Bebé holder
44. Poet's before
48. In the heavens
50. Mind terribly
51. Give up
52. Communist leader Zhou ___
53. Kind of pad or pool
54. Up to the present
57. Earthenware jar
58. Julia of Hollywood
59. Bahrain biggie
60. Corddry of "Studio 60 on the Sunset Strip"
61. Building location
62. Tigers foe

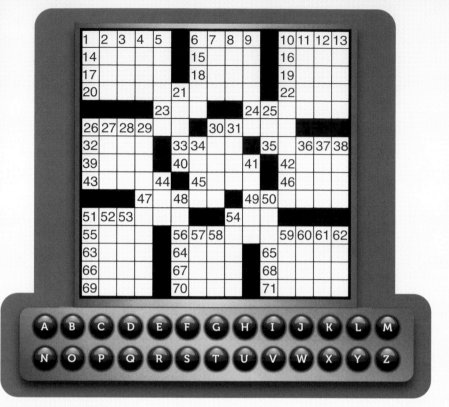

Watch What You Say

Across

1. Didn't take part, with "out"
6. The Crimson Tide, to fans
10. Misses
14. "Keen!"
15. Old Glory, for one
16. Not fantastic
17. Stop with
18. She gets what she wants
19. Queens's ___ Stadium
20. Old married folks?
22. Do, say
23. Null service
24. "Cut that out!"
26. Iron output
30. Court activity
32. Director Kazan
33. Quiz answer
35. Finds fault
39. Pickled delicacies
40. Stable dads
42. Page
43. Where the mouth is
45. Musical finale
46. Certain something
47. Cupid's dart
49. Fossil preserver
51. "___ Kate"
54. Diana Ross musical, with "The"
55. Type of history
56. They watch what you say
63. Painter Magritte
64. Peace Nobelist Wiesel
65. On the up and up
66. Fork over, with "up"
67. Ship of Columbus
68. ___ Gay (WWII plane)
69. Tide type
70. Furniture wood
71. Thing of value

Down

1. Your
2. Confined
3. "There!"

4. Series ender
5. "Go on!"
6. Black key on a piano
7. Gobs
8. Kind of bonding
9. Tennis great Andre
10. Tavern for health nuts?
11. Fable fellow
12. "Chicago Hope" actress Christine
13. Slushy stuff
21. Track events
25. Center X or O
26. Herbicide target
27. Protected from the wind
28. All you can eat
29. Like a quick somnambulist?
30. "Presumed Innocent" author Scott
31. English horn, for one
34. "Little Caesar" gangster
36. Enlist again
37. Start for scope or meter
38. Petty quarrel
41. Composer Erik
44. Hurler's asset
48. Ease up
50. Showy shrub
51. Islam's sacred text
52. Castle of many steps
53. Rooftop visitor
54. Unleash
57. "Would ___ to you?"
58. Colada fruit
59. Retreats
60. Some stars have big ones
61. Stir up, without a spoon
62. RBI, for one

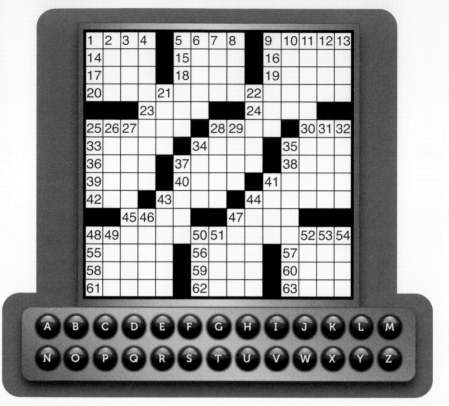

Presidential Portraits

Across

1. Yawn-inducing
5. Wren or hen
9. Mushroom cloud maker
14. College in New Rochelle
15. Buffalo's lake
16. Palmer, to pals
17. Collette of "In Her Shoes"
18. Zip
19. Championship
20. First jug at the bar?
23. Failures, in slang
24. Small pooch, briefly
25. Polyester brand
28. Nicholas or Peter
30. Stylish, once
33. Online sales
34. Opportunities for repentance
35. Granada greeting
36. Suffix with Congo
37. Great grade
38. Group of soldiers
39. "The Wizard of Oz" actor
40. One of the Brady Bunch
41. Tylenol alternative
42. Football's Parseghian
43. Methods
44. Took part in the game
45. "Say no more!"
47. Goes out with
48. Storage of angling gear?
55. Ward off
56. Per unit
57. Couple, in a column
58. Joiner's phrase
59. Fidel's brother
60. Forum home
61. City on the Ruhr
62. Prime the poker pot
63. High-tech: suf.

Down

1. They may be boring
2. Rifle
3. Visitor to Siam
4. Source of hot air

114

5. Harmless
6. Fairway choices
7. One year in a trunk
8. Heartfelt
9. Carroll's mad tea drinker
10. Building unit
11. Where to see presidential portraits?
12. Denver's elevation, roughly
13. Brewski
21. Screwdriver, e.g.
22. "No, thanks"
25. Perry's secretary
26. On ___ (rampaging)
27. The ability to sing and play guitar, to Johnny?
28. Scrabble pieces
29. Cozy
31. Kind of drab
32. Passé
34. Full of pep
35. Island attire
37. Yawning
41. Obi-Wan player
43. Chinese dumpling
44. Tune from "Funny Girl"
46. Pang
47. Pub potable
48. Celebrity
49. Currier's partner
50. Fictional Georgia plantation
51. Bridge
52. Part of Ripley's phrase
53. Nautilus commander
54. Feds

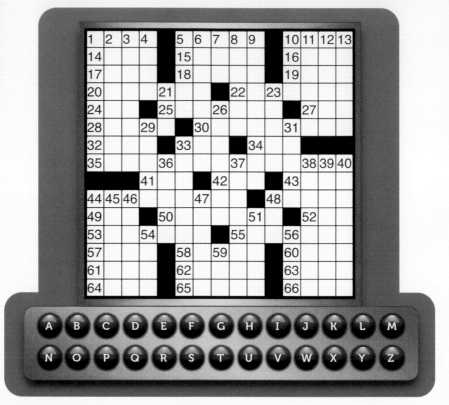

Frequent Flier

Across

1. Chess win
5. Oodles
10. Does sums
14. Aid in crime
15. Playwright Edward
16. Robert Frost work, e.g.
17. Printed matter
18. Tribute with friendly insults
19. Preminger or Klemperer
20. Severe shocks
22. When fewer people are online, e.g.
24. Surgery sites: abbr.
25. Sluggishness
27. What a polygraph test may reveal
28. Furnish food
30. What trick-or-treaters push
32. ___-jerk reaction
33. "My Big Fat Greek Wedding" actress Vardalos
34. Suffix with profit or racket
35. Frequent flier?
41. Response to "Are you?"
42. Owl's cry
43. Is unable to
44. Spot
48. Caterpillar or grub
49. Fuss and bother
50. Get really close
52. German article
53. Minuteman's enemy
55. A con artist pulls this
57. Tickled-pink feeling
58. They make trumpets less loud
60. Grandson of Adam
61. Pipe elbows
62. Wipe away
63. Thompson of "The Remains of the Day"
64. Take a load off
65. Groups that broke away
66. Bird abode

Down

1. Digging tools similar to pickaxes
2. Different from normal behavior
3. Oil, in "The Ballad of Jed Clampett"
4. "___, Brute?"
5. Plastic wrap brand
6. Neared, with "on"
7. Lawyers' grp.
8. Spaniard who explored the Mississippi
9. Ignite
10. Each, in pricing
11. "This I gotta hear!"
12. Minor point
13. Prepares ham
21. Former Russian orbiter
23. Name on a pencil
26. Driver who won't let you pass
29. Causing goosebumps
31. Kane of "All My Children"
33. Get specific about people
36. Final word
37. Folk music gathering, e.g.
38. "So sorry"
39. Makes poisonous
40. Eyes rudely
44. ___-than-life
45. "Let's Eat Right to Keep Fit" author Davis
46. Sings in the Alps, perhaps
47. Junction with surgeon's stitches
48. Bandleader Brown
51. Operates with a beam
54. "___ la vie"
56. Last year's twelve-year-old
59. Tic-___-toe

Who Swallowed the Canary?

Across

1. More than passes
5. Truth ___
10. Somewhat
14. Body partner
15. Treasured instrument
16. Wise guy
17. Damsel's deliverer
18. Dietetic, on packages
19. Pelt
20. Stuff on a poultry farmer's shoes?
23. Dermal opening
24. Rival of Helena
25. Parachute part
28. Breakfast sweet
31. Came to
32. Baseball blooper
33. Potato feature
36. Take off
37. "Move it!"
38. ___-à-porter (ready-to-wear clothes)
39. Night school subj.
40. Oil industry honcho
41. Not work very hard
42. Stop talking
44. Flower child, e.g.
45. In conflict with, with "of"
47. Term of politeness
48. Evidence of swallowing the canary?
54. Air resistance
55. Cricket sound
56. Seeks damages
58. To be, in France
59. Grocery section
60. Sarcastic response
61. Comedian Foxx
62. Fall blossom
63. Dogpatch creator

Down

1. Lenten symbol
2. Future alumna
3. Coin on the Continent

4. Slug
5. Pay
6. Chew the scenery
7. Whole slew
8. Nevada neighbor
9. Little bug
10. Judge
11. Put up with Eminem's songs?
12. Light-footed
13. Not quite bright
21. Terse refusal
22. Name in a will
25. Outdoor eatery
26. Boring tools
27. Christmas chicken?
28. Hang down

29. Memphis middle name
30. "That's ___ my problem"
32. Pale brown
34. Sammy Davis' "___ Can"
35. Cigar ending
37. Mil. defense weapon
38. Songs for teens
40. Island in Indonesia
41. "I'm history!"
43. Did a fencer's move
44. Clothes receptacle
45. Pocket calculator, e.g.
46. Cup of tea
47. Haggard of country music
49. Mar. Madness source
50. Not just one of those things

51. High school subj.
52. Big horn
53. Dickens' Uriah
57. Indy 500 logo

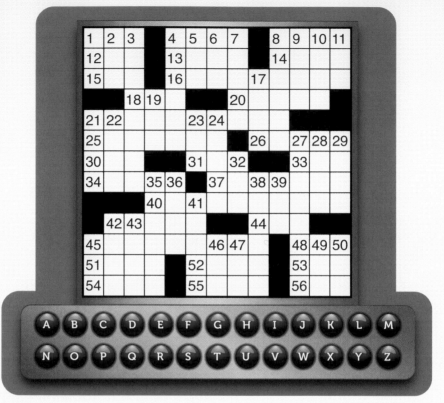

Tree Tops

Across

1. Gossip
4. Self-righteous person
8. ___ jure (by the law itself)
12. Hurry-scurry
13. Heckelphone cousin
14. Housekeeper
15. Body of lawyers
16. Colonial symbol of hospitality
18. Flightless bird
20. Certain bead make up
21. Leader with no responsibilities
25. Resistance to change
26. Safecrackers
30. Uplifting attire
31. Shoot down
33. Sénat vote?
34. Montenegro dwellers
37. Frog variety
40. Popular name for a home-repair product
42. Sudden attack
44. Drivel
45. Rubbery candy
48. Maryland's state tree
51. "My Girl" star Chlumsky
52. It may be a penny
53. Yonder yacht
54. Peel off
55. June 6, 1944
56. Graffiti signature

Down

1. Quick punch
2. Oklahoma headquarters of the Chickasaw Nation
3. Drive in the form of a screw
4. Roy Lichtenstein's genre
5. What you get for driving someone home: abbr.
6. Former Romanian president Iliescu
7. Amelia and Abigail Gabble in "The Aristocats"
8. Prevent
9. He got a brand new bag, in song
10. Reservoir deposit

11. Poetic tribute

17. Not toward

19. Dickens's "___ Mutual Friend"

21. Misinformation pieces

22. Concerning

23. Teutonic article

24. First name in Rastafari movement

27. One of four on a football field

28. Mentor

29. Competing team

32. Gen ___

35. Nickname giver on ESPN

36. Dispatch

38. Large bird of prey

39. European Tour grp.

41. Substitute for "mea culpa"

42. Grand ___ Railroad

43. Dodge car

45. Subject of Boyle's law

46. Stop running

47. "One Day ___ Time" (TV series)

49. Epiphany exclamation

50. Beer container

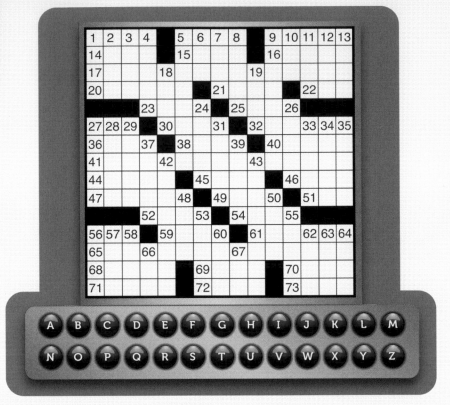

Grammar School

Across

1. "Buona ____ " (Italian greeting)
5. Some are green
9. Recidivate
14. Valhalla V.I.P.
15. Ill-considered
16. Homeric tale
17. The real McCoy?
20. Deficiency of red blood cells
21. Soothing stuff
22. Barbie's beau
23. Obsolete Pakistani currency
25. Ready
27. Lizard, old-style
30. Baker's dozen?
32. Someone who raves
36. Anchor
38. Vault
40. Effectively cut short
41. Third from last
44. Epitome
45. General Sherman is a huge one
46. Breezed through
47. ____ Day, August 1
49. Ball material
51. "Don't give up!"
52. Mark left by Zorro?
54. Barber's job
56. Can. neighbor
59. Diva's delivery
61. Points on a map with equal barometric pressure
65. To badly speak of one?
68. Glue
69. Was philanthropic
70. Kind of wire
71. Was available for stud
72. Smeltery input
73. "What are the ____ ?"

Down

1. Scotch's partner
2. Biblical plot
3. Abounding
4. The inner self (Jung)
5. Percussion instrument

6. "Dig in!"
7. In the Red?
8. Characteristic of a mudstone
9. The learned
10. Foreman's superior
11. Basketball maneuver
12. Ad headline
13. Heaven on Earth
18. Opening time, maybe
19. Guffaw
24. 007?
26. Bottom line in medical treatment?
27. Spam container
28. Henry, Jane, or Peter
29. Emblematic pole

31. Long-beaked fish of temperate Atlantic waters
33. Piece of land
34. Organic compound
35. Long and slender
37. Large quantity of written matter
39. Plicate
42. Mollified
43. Earthenware casserole dishes
48. Hindu wrap
50. Not final or absolute
53. Beatle
55. Guiding principle

56. Ind. fed. agency for mail processing and delivery
57. Run-in
58. To boot
60. Winston Churchill's "____ Country"
62. Shuttlecock
63. All fired up
64. Gym set
66. Four-time Japanese prime minister
67. "____ Got a Secret"

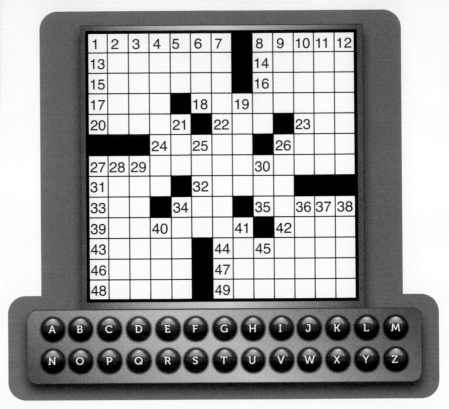

Manly Names

Across

1. Dodge traffic, perhaps
8. Narrow estuary
13. Momentum
14. Goodbye, maybe
15. South American hero
16. Three-masted ship
17. "Monday Night Football" network
18. Old stereo component
20. Classroom sights
22. Pennington and Cobb
23. Cambodian currency
24. Vieira's cohost
26. Boot base
27. Befitting a blackguard
31. Paella ingredient
32. One member of Houston's NFL team
33. Bird with a snood
34. Foot, to Flavius
35. Leia strangled him
39. Small, as a town
42. Like many basketball players
43. Devonshire dad
44. A number that designates place
46. Patronized a certain restaurant
47. State of perfect inner peace
48. Finds peace
49. Scanner dial

Down

1. Sudden shift while sailing
2. Narrow winning margin
3. Short shouts
4. Dermal features
5. Off-road ride: abbr.
6. Bloody Mary's daughter
7. Mr. Miyagi's gift to Daniel
8. Documents sent by phone
9. "____ Three Lives"
10. Actor Paul in the College Football Hall of Fame
11. Jennifer Lopez movie
12. High-stepping horse

19. Corning glass
21. ____ Marino
25. Speak
26. Having healing powers
27. At an acceptable level
28. Recent delivery
29. Oogenesis products
30. Capt.'s superior
34. Where cables connect
36. Uninspiring
37. Maillot ____ (Tour de France jersey for younger competitors)
38. Sufism deity
40. Preliminary race
41. "Coming to America" actor La Salle
45. ____ Hill (music group)

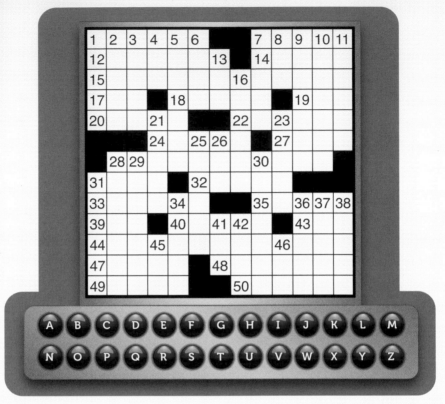

All for Naught

Across

1. Fixes
7. Tanks and such
12. Good places for basking
14. Gina's good
15. Swish shot
17. Mancinetti opera "___ e Leandro"
18. Turns sharply
19. Work on roots, perhaps
20. Parisian tenant's payment
22. Harder to grasp
24. Texas shrub
27. Grasslands
28. Post office request
31. Off-white
32. Preminger and von Bismarck
33. Walking
35. Stares
39. Big initials in old films
40. Enterprise communications officer
43. Phone menu no.
44. Harsh policy
47. Space shuttle part
48. Play during the day
49. Rejoinder in a kids' argument
50. "Grease" high school

Down

1. "Lou Grant" star
2. Poet Marianne
3. John with a piano
4. Slangy dissent
5. Kind of window
6. Trigonometry function
7. Maltreatment
8. Monotonous practice
9. French exclamation
10. Like many leases
11. Olympic judges
13. Actuarial datum
16. Chicken piece
21. Universal donor
23. Peruvian novelist Mario Vargas ___
25. Mythical threadspinner

26. Soundstage cry
28. Screaming Yellow ___
29. Facing severe punishment
30. History teacher in the "Luann" comic strip
31. Russian wolfhound
34. Expenses
36. Pasta with diagonally cut ends
37. Win laurels
38. Sharpening device
41. German city on the Danube
42. Adjective in a Hitchcock title
45. "Season of Glass" singer
46. Legal follower

Crossword Titles